Police Pursuit

— OF THE —

Common Good

Reforming & Restoring
Police Community

GINGER CHARLES, PH.D.

(ret. Police Sergeant)

CO-AUTHORED
Leadership Resilience: Lessons for Leaders from the Policing Frontline

BALBOA.
PRESS

A DIVISION OF HAY HOUSE

North East Multi-Regional Training
-Instructors' Library-
355 Smoke Tree Plaza
North Aurora, IL 60542

Balboa Press books may be ordered through booksellers or by contacting:

Balboa Press
A Division of Hay House
1663 Liberty Drive
Bloomington, IN 47403
www.balboapress.com
1 (877) 407-4847

Cover illustration: Jamie Villanueva

Print information available on the last page.

ISBN: 978-1-5043-5294-9 (sc)
ISBN: 978-1-5043-5296-3 (hc)
ISBN: 978-1-5043-5295-6 (e)

Library of Congress Control Number: 2016903901

Balboa Press rev. date: 3/15/2016

When I began to write this book, I wondered about what it would say to my peers in law enforcement, to other communities, to family and friends. On a larger scale, could the book "help" us work toward a resolution in our police organizations and marginalized communities? So, how will I write this book? I know this … I will make some angry. But our anger can help us move in new directions of growth and change.

In 1998, I remember listening to Arun Gandhi, Mahatma Gandhi's grandson, as he explained his grandfather's message about anger. He said "anger is like electricity, neither good nor bad, it is simply energy. It is our choice how we use this energy or electricity." If the book creates anger, it is my intention to move us into a higher level of understanding for all of us, those in law enforcement, those served by law enforcement, each one of us.

And so, I write this book from a position as a police officer and a research psychologist, believing both provide a unique lived experience through this topic. I have spent most of my adult life as a police officer. Therefore, my time and experiences in police work give me a solid ability to understand what I am exploring and defining in the police culture. I understand the police perspective because I was a police officer.

During my time as a police officer, I worked on my education, attaining my graduate degrees. I then added "research psychologist" to my skills and abilities, believing that a research perspective "within" the police culture may provide valuable information about that culture and its health. There is still very little research within the police culture. This is due to a variety of factors, one being the secrecy of its members.

I started my career as a police officer in 1986 in a very small Colorado mountain town. I left this police department after serving over 10 years and moved to the sixth largest police agency in the Denver metro area. I worked in that community for about 16 years, totaling 27 years as a police officer when I retired in April 2013. In between my employment with these two police organizations, I worked for a short time (11 months) with the Colorado State Patrol.

Throughout my entire law enforcement career, I was fascinated with behavior; behavior of cops, of the communities we serve, criminals, and people in general. That spurred my quest to go back to school and get my masters degree in Clinical Psychology and eventually my doctorate in Health Psychology. I decided early in my academic pursuit that I was not a clinician. That is not my temperament. I am a researcher. I research and write about police officers, their health risk factors, resiliency in police work, and how to help our police communities. My research focuses on what police officers do well in their lives in order to survive and thrive in police work.

There are so many police officers that do great work, who understand what it means to work in this profession, and who care deeply about our two goals of preventing crime and protecting lives. This book is written for them and their integrity, faith, and service. My intention is to help these police officers restore their community and culture. It is my goal to provide a path for new police officers to begin and maintain a healthy police career. Finally, I hope to encourage those that do not care nor honor police service to leave the profession.

What I know is we cannot move forward until we understand where we have been. So let us stop and look around. Let us see where we stand. We must objectively look at our behavior and form a plan to fix this fracture and conflict between our police community and those communities served. This is a gentle persuasion to have a deeper dialogue about what must change for us in our police communities.

Make no mistake, police must change, and that does not mean weakness. In fact, looking at our behavior and making adjustments is key to our survival and adaptability. That which does not change or refuses to change will eventually die and disappear. Please walk with me as we explore who we are in police work, why we behave the way we do, and why we should and must change. These questions are imperative to the health of each police officer in the United States and our communities that we serve. This book is not about blame or defending a side. It is about responsibility.

The language in this book uses the pronoun "we" when I describe police officers, their behavior, and experiences. I am retired from police work, yet I have been a cop for over half of my life. I have been truly ingrained in the profession of policing. I love police work. I love all law enforcement and consider them my family. What I know is all our families are flawed and part of healing with family is our ability to identify the flaws and work to minimize their impact on our relationships with others.

Because I have aligned with police work, I use "we." I have made some of the same mistakes that I illustrate in this book. I am flawed as well. I may have expertise in this area of research but I am working on being an expert. When we think of experts we think they make no mistakes or relatively few. However the truth is, the mistakes made by experts are so small the audience cannot see those mistakes anymore. That is an expert. That is what I am wanting for the law enforcement community: to practice and practice, to improve on our mistakes so those mistakes become invisible to our communities we serve. We are human beings and we make mistakes. We are humans interacting with each other and I am part of the "we" in law enforcement.

So the book is a look at what is happening in the police community. Why is there such conflict between the police community and marginalized communities happening all over the United States? The conflict is not localized. Why is this happening now and why so pronounced? We cannot blame the shootings, riots, clashes, and errant behavior within police communities on just one state going awry. It is everywhere, it is obvious, and it is not going away until we look at this problem. So let us begin with a quote from John F Kennedy on the day after the assassination of Dr. Martin Luther King, Jr.:

Whenever any American's life is taken by another American unnecessarily-Whether it is done in the name of the law or in the defiance of law, by one man or a gang, in cold blood or in passion, in an attack of violence or in response to violence – whenever we tear at the fabric of life which another man has painfully and clumsily woven for himself and his children, the whole nation is degraded ... Yet we seemingly tolerate a rising level of violence that ignores our common humanity and our claims to civilization alike. We calmly accept newspaper reports of civilian slaughter in far off lands. We glorify killing on movie and television screens and call it enter-tainment. We make it easy for men of all shades of sanity to acquire weapons and ammunition they desire ... Too often we honor swagger and bluster and the wielders of force; too often we excuse those who are willing to build their own lives on the shattered dreams of others. Some Americans who preach non-violence abroad fail to practice it here at home. Some who accuse others of incit-ing riots have by their own conduct invited them. Some look for scapegoats, others look for conspiracies, but this much is clear; violence breeds violence, repression brings retaliations, and only a cleaning of our whole society can remove this sickness from our soul. (Kennedy, 1968)

The year is now 2016. How far have we come? It is time to look at our behavior in our police community and find solutions to our conflicts.

ACKNOWLEDGMENTS

I must thank those four or five police officers that taught me how to be a good cop, to serve the community with integrity, to honor the public's trust and the badge that I had been given in 1986. These men helped me understand this profession is one of the highest ways to serve humankind.

I also want to thank four women in the psychology department at Modesto Junior College, Modesto, California: Dr. Lisa Carlstrom, Dr. Shelly Fichtenkort, Professor Rebecca Ganes, and Professor Lee Kooler. These women gave me the opportunity to serve at Modesto Junior College. They guided and gave me advice in teaching students the subject of psychology through a lived experience.

I wish to thank my dean, Dr. Jennifer Hamilton, at Modesto Junior College for her constant words of encouragement to all faculty members in her division. She demonstrates the traits of true leadership: offering guidance and direction as well as encouraging the creative freedom of the teaching process.

I am indebted to the individuals interviewed in this book. They are part of the solution. To my niece, Jamie Villanueva, I thank you for the beautiful cover art you have drawn for this book. Finally, many thanks go to my mother, Marian Charles, who was a reader and part time editor during the development of the book. Each of you has helped me write this book and I am grateful.

This book is dedicated to
Great, Great Grandmother GALLAGHER
She was brave
She was a survivor
She is an unknown Heroine
And I do not know her first name

CONTENTS

Preface v

Acknowledgments ix

Chapter 1: Introduction 1

Chapter 2: Understanding the Problem. 7
Identifying a "tipping point" 9
Never Giving Up Ground. 14
De-Escalation. 16

Chapter 3: Social Psychology & a Culture of Evil 20
Social psychological effects in policing 24
Dispositional vs. Situational Attribution Theory. 26
Aggression. 30
Prejudice and Implicit Bias. 34
Groups 37

Chapter 4: Policing as a "Business" 40
CompStat. 44
Managing vs. Leading 47
Egoic Goals 48
Lowering of Standards. 51

Chapter 5: Stress & Service 54
Burnout & Compassion Fatigue 60
Post-Traumatic Stress Disorder 61
Psychology of Police 64

Chapter 6: Compassion & Re-engagement 69
Importance of Compassion 69
Forgiveness 73
Challenge & Change of Police 75
Systemic vs. Individual Changes 77

Chapter 7: How Do You Want to Be Policed? 80
Barry Graves 82
Professor Albert Smith 88
M.E.Ch.A. 93
Common emerging themes 98

Chapter 8: Solutions for Our Police Community 104
Individual & Systemic Reformation 104
Toward Resilience 109
Integrity 111
Awaken the Spiritual Warrior 116
Mentoring 118

Chapter 9: Conclusion 127

Bibliography 134

CHAPTER 1

Introduction

"Darkness cannot drive out darkness; only light can do that.
Hate cannot drive out hate; only love can do that."
—Dr. Martin Luther King Jr.

The history of law enforcement began with captured Nubian slaves in Mesopotamia. These slaves were considered the first police force and were used as praetorian guards, marketplace watchmen, or mercenaries (Berg, 1998). I have always found the early history of police interesting, particularly when we examine current issues in our police communities and the conflict with marginalized communities. Our history in law enforcement tends to demonstrate that we (police officers) come from marginalized communities as well.

In the thirteenth and sixteenth centuries, "night watchman" and the "rattle patrol" were used to protect merchants from vagrants and thievery. As cities expanded and people congregated, those who were privileged needed individuals to protect their belongings and property. Some of these night watchmen were punished for their own crimes and assigned as night watchmen as atonement. Many times I have heard police officers say, "To be a good cop, you have to think like a criminal." Certainly this behavior appears to be part of our history.

Yet we evolved out of this behavior and early beginnings to become more professional, thanks, in part, to Sir Robert Peel. In 1829,

Sir Robert Peel was instrumental in the passage of the Metropolitan Police Act in England, which created a new police force of men who were professional, educated, and disciplined. We in the United States began to follow the "Peel Principles" of law enforcement in the nineteenth century. However, this was also during a time of race and industrial riots involving Irish immigrants and Native Americans. Police were trained to think they were better than the working class, which instigated conflict between police and community. Yet most of these officers were recruited from this very same culture. Here is the beginning of conflict with who we are and whom we serve.

Perhaps if we view our history of law enforcement by looking at our behavior from the beginning to the present, we might discover patterns of conduct that help identify why we are experiencing such violence today. Additionally, we can look at police behavior from a social psychological perspective as a way of understanding that behavior, recognizing that our behavior can change when we actually view its effect in society and various situations. Finally, by examining police behavior from our earliest beginnings to today, we are afforded the opportunity to change the behavior because we have observed those patterns through our history.

In our evolution and adaptation, two law enforcement goals in the United States are paramount to good policing. The first is *the prevention of crime and disorder and the preservation of peace.* The second goal for law enforcement officers is *the protection of life, property, and personal liberty.* So what is currently happening in the United States with police and society?

There has been a clear demonstration in the United States since 2013 that our police culture has a significant problem. Some moments in history appear to demand change, and I believe we are experiencing one of those moments. If we choose to ignore these moments or don't deal with them ethically, they shall rise again in intensity and quantity. This has occurred within the police culture and community over and over, until today we have reached a tipping point: our police community is under the microscope, the public trust has been severely damaged, and many of our communities are demanding change.

Earlier incidents have certainly illustrated the tension between law enforcement and marginalized communities. Look no further than the time of the Civil Rights Movement to see the tremendous clashes between "people of color" and law enforcement. What has changed from that time to the present day? There were changes to laws and guidelines. People were forced to integrate.

Yet, most people were angry about integration and change. It did not matter whether it was the individuals forced to integrate or the individuals "accepting" the integrated person. Everyone was uncomfortable, familiarity was gone, isolation increased, resentment and divisiveness became pronounced. This example in our history illustrates our inability to "teach" each other through these critical events, such as integration. It is typical of us to simply "tell" our communities that they must change, "force" or impose new laws without much explanation, and then fail to educate when punishment is easier.

In my opinion, our process of educating people about civil rights and integration was basic, reactive rather than reflective. In the United States, we still have not done a good job of actually teaching people how to integrate. We have enforced/demanded and punished people into integration. Clearly, this approach only fosters tension and conflict. Changing ourselves at the cellular level to find acceptance with each other requires time and work on every individual's part. But it also requires money, so instead of truly taking the time to explain why we must change, we institute laws and rules to enforce our new behaviors while underneath, the issue of inequality remains and may be passed down through generations and families on both sides of the issue.

So we are still faced with the issues of inequality, racism, and marginalized communities. The police community usually is the first place where this conflict begins to show. When tension and frustration reach a boiling point, the police are often the first to encounter that frustration. Because, unfortunately, the police community is also at a breaking point, when conflicts with marginalized communities arise.

As a nation, we demand that our law enforcement officers confront human destructiveness and suffering, defend our communities, and stand between chaos and order. All of these demands necessitate a unique type of individual. If police officers experience isolation, feel undervalued, or suffer from the effects of stress, then we cannot protect and serve our communities. In fact, a dysfunctional environment may provide the perfect opportunity for corruption and violence within our police culture and towards community.

The police community is currently facing a crisis of spirit—the loss of meaning and purpose. This is apparent from the extensive friction we have seen between our police officers and communities. The behavior does not represent a healthy environment. When reviewing the shooting in Ferguson, Missouri, and the choking death of Eric Garner in New York, FBI Director James Comey has described our law enforcement community in the United States as at a crossroads.

The city of Baltimore has also experienced a significant increase in activism, rioting, and unrest since the death of Freddy Gray. He was chased by officers and then arrested. At some point during the arrest, his spine snapped. He was then put inside a police transport van unrestrained. Freddy Gray asked for medical help and then quickly fell into a coma. His death in April 2015 has been described as "revealing a rupture" in the city, where protests grew and violence increased for several weeks (Wallace-Wells, 2015). Currently, six police officers are under indictment for several criminal charges, including murder.

Unfortunately, we have seen many more recent examples of police violence and corruption. More recent is the Chicago Police Department's issues with charging one of their own, Jason Van Dyke, for first-degree murder. In 2014, Van Dyke shot a young black male sixteen times. The young male was armed with a knife but was not approaching the officers. Several officers were on scene with Van Dyke and did not fire their weapons, but some reported that the male approached the officers with the knife, contrary to the captured video. According to news reports, Van Dyke had at least twenty use-of-force complaints since 2002. Three of those complaints were for excessive force, yet no discipline was given.

With the current and continual confrontation between police and marginalized communities, the levels of stress and distress in the profession, and the hidden layers of corruption and inequality in our police organizations, police officers may have lost meaning in their profession. Officers who have detached from humanistic pursuits can become mechanistic, cold, and calloused. When the organization does not care for police officers, we (police) do not have the capacity to care for those we serve.

In an article entitled *Seven Reasons Police Brutality is Systemic, Not Anecdotal*, Kristian (2014) states that many departments do not provide sufficient training for police officers in non-violent situations. Additionally, the standards of what constitutes excessive force or brutality vary from agency to agency and state to state. When an officer is found to be at fault for some type of misconduct, the consequences are usually minimal. It then becomes the responsibility of the taxpayer to pay for the settlement for any police misconduct. Kristian (2014) notes that police militarization and the targeting of minorities add to systemic brutality as well. Finally, the police culture itself reports that misconduct is very widespread.

The Department of Justice reported that 84 percent of police officers have observed other officers using excessive force on community members. Sixty-one percent of those officers admitted that they did not report the use of force. During my experience as a police officer, I witnessed another police officer using excessive force. I reported that force without hesitation, as it was morally right to do so and it was the law. I remember that my police chief and the assistant chief were very concerned about my safety, fearing retaliation by the police community.

So there are several issues facing our police communities. Additionally, there are a multitude of reasons to address these issues.

The current problems and events unfolding in our communities and police culture are the coalescing opportunity to correct what is happening. Finally, our work together to change this in our communities provides the opportunity for all of us to work towards health and wholeness in our world. I am a firm believer that if our police officers are healthy and thriving, they will be the first contact with those they serve who may be in crisis. By educating and disciplining without brutality, they can create further healing in the communities, promoting humanism and compassion.

Our police culture can choose to react to the current issues and find some temporary solution to bandage the gaping wound between the police and the communities they serve. If our police organizations decide to find a quick fix, the issues we are currently facing will resurface again. In fact, it is highly likely that the conflict between our police and communities will be even more violent and disturbing than what we are currently experiencing. We have a choice to look at long-term solutions to the conflicts before us. We have never been challenged to fix these issues of violence and conflict as we are today. It is imperative that we explore healing resolutions for our communities and our police officers.

I am repeating an earlier point. This book is not about assigning blame or finding fault with anyone. Blaming or finding fault only creates tension, which inhibits learning. This is about responsibility. This is about demonstrating why it is good for law enforcement to change.

Finally, I am incorporating questions for the reader throughout the following chapters. It offers the reader an opportunity to apply the information from the book and evaluate whether that information provides insights or further discussions. They are simply another tool to use or ignore.

CHAPTER 2

Understanding the Problem

*"He who fights monsters might take care lest he
thereby become a monster. And if you gaze for long
into an abyss, the abyss gazes also into you."*
Friedrich Nietzsche

The problem before us in the police community is the increasing number of violent police contacts involving marginalized communities. What was the tipping point when the violence in our police culture became so pronounced? This may be impossible to pin down. However, let us walk back to New Years Day 2009 and the fatal shooting of Oscar Grant at the Fruitvale BART (Bay Area Rapid Transit) station in Oakland, California. The end result of this conflict is the police officer mistook his handgun for his taser and he shot and killed Oscar Grant. The police officer was charged and convicted of manslaughter.

After an investigation, other officers were fired and the Chief of Police of the BART transit system resigned. The fatal shooting is the final snapshot in a disturbing video between law enforcement and that marginalized community. This is significant as it did not appear that the officer's intent was to kill Grant but the officer was still held accountable for his mistake. His actions caused the death of Grant. Use of force experts later determined the officer's mistake to be a substantial training problem as the officer's taser was carried on the same side as his firearm. However, the case is memorable because, regardless of intent, it demonstrated a significant conflict between the police and a marginalized community. The incident may have shown the development of a problem between police and community.

Cellphone videos showed an angry encounter between police officers and Oscar Grant and his friends. So what was the precipitating event? Many readers will have their own idea of what "caused" the final shooting. Again, all participants in the event have responsibility in the event. But what could be changed? This question may allow us to explore the root of the problem rather than blaming one group or individual.

According to Webster's Dictionary, the defintion of "marginalized" communities is "to treat a person, group, or concept as insignificant or peripheral." Marginalized communities are made up of individuals who are between their original culture and the new culture they are trying to assimilate. Some of the reasons these individuals remain inbetween cultures can be lack of acceptance, lack of resources (financial), and lack of understanding between the culture and the individual, which may be very painful for people who are in these marginalized communities. Often, resources are limited and the lack of understanding about how to integrate and become part of the culture can be illusive. Additionally, the marginalized culture may perpetuate itself generation after generation.

We should remember, police officers did not create these marginalized communities. These communities are created by inequities in our government, society, and economy. However, law enforcement may foster marginalization by enforcement actions and inequitable or unjust beliefs. When human beings group together and become a community, there are always those "outside" of the community who desire to be in the community. From a social psychological perspective, this behavior has been around since humans have gathered together in groups. The police are there to preserve peace and protect life. And, many times there are variables that interfere with police accomplishing these two goals. Many of those variables are created by the dysfunction of the police culture.

In October 2015, there were over 800 police shootings in the United States. But before we attack that number, let's look closer. Many of these shootings were justified uses of force, such as officers responding to deadly force and shooting to protect their lives or the lives of others. For example, police officers responding to the mass shooting at the Navy Recruiting office, the many school shootings, or deadly force events at theatres represent justified uses of deadly force. In addition, there are those shootings where police officers were faced with lethal force and must defend themselves. These are obvious and appropriate uses of force. Only five percent of these 800 police shootings are considered questionable.

There are over 655,000 police officers/law enforcement officers in the United States. Additionally, there are over 100,000 Federal officers. To date, there are less than ten police officers who currently have been charged with murder. While there is much debate about whether other police officers should have or could have been charged with murder, the numbers illustrate that we are looking at the "outliers" when exploring this tragic problem in our communities. However, the "outliers" are very important from a research perspective and can shift our world, demanding attention.

So why should we pay attention to the "outliers" if only five percent of police shootings are questionable? Outliers are people or things that are found outside a defined area or organization. These outliers can be significant in any study, revealing to the researcher the actual important issue being explored. There is a great amount of information we can acquire by looking at these outliers because they can illustrate a problem in a group prior to or without affecting the whole group. However, the entire police community is feeling the effect of the outlying behavior.

Identifying a "tipping point"

Current trends in the media since 2013 have reported case after case of questionable to criminal behavior perpetrated upon communities by police. However, there has been questionable behavior in the police community since policing started. As stated earlier, our origins in policing reveal that some individuals were "punished" for petty crimes by being assigned to work the "rattle patrol" checking businesses and preventing crime. This was their penance, to serve and protect their victims in the community.

In the 1970's, Frank Serpico revealed the mass corruption of police officers in New York City Police Department. This certainly did not stop corruption in the largest police department in the United States. In fact, Serpico left the police force after being shot in the face, testifying at the Knapp Commission, and then moved to Switzerland. When he resigned from the New York Police Department, he made several suggestions to the Knapp commission about how to end the corruption in the police department. The most important of those ideas about preventing corruption was to recognize that police cannot police themselves.

NYPD experienced another major hit of corruption in the 1980's and 1990's. In 1986, several officers in the 77th precinct were arrested and fired for corruption: burglary, theft, racketeering, and other criminal events. Members of the 75th precinct who were involved in corruption and crime watched and learned how the police department addressed the corrupt behavior at the 77th precinct. Many of those officers resigned from the police department before they were charged with any crime. However, one police officer chose to take his chances and stayed until he was investigated and arrested for multiple crimes, to include conspiracy to commit murder (Dowd, 2015).

It is not my intention to disparage the New York Police Department in this book. I am confident that there are many honest, compassionate, dedicated police officers in this police organization. Nevertheless, the largest police department in the country provides a multitude of examples for this book.

We have seen the same types of corruption in the New Orleans Police Department. There were several officers arrested and charged for racketeering, burglary, drug offenses, and even murder. Between

1997 and 2000, Los Angeles Police Department investigated their CRASH unit (Community Resources Against Street Hoodlums) in the Rampart Division. The investigation began when one undercover LAPD officer shot and killed another officer, who was off duty at the time in an apparent road rage incident. This was LAPD's tipping point; a recognition there was something wrong in this division. The issue of police corruption is not isolated to one part of the country but rather simmers below the surface of many, if not all, law enforcement organizations until the corruption reveals itself usually in the most public way.

Examining the documentary *The Seven Five*, Michael Dowd described his corrupt police career in the New York Police Department. Some of his insights into his criminal behavior illustrated how corruption can weave itself into the fabric of the police profession. Dowd (2015) described he tested to be a "cop" but had no direction. He clearly stated he had no sense of service. Dowd explained that he had some integrity training while in the academy. However, he admitted that he, his fellow officers, and his training officers did not take that training seriously. He detailed that this time in the academy was important for him and his peers to learn how to "cover their ass."

Michael Dowd (2015) described to the investigatory board what it meant to be a "good cop." He said, "You never give up another cop," and it is important to "back another cop one hundred percent because he is your back-up." Dowd stated that if you did not support your peers and back them, you might not have any back-up when you were on the streets in a dangerous situation. So the pressure to "assimilate" to the police culture is tremendous, particularly when there are significant value differences between the individual and the police culture.

Yet, there are those police officers in the New York Police Department as well as other police organizations that do not succumb to this pressure. Those who enter the profession with a sense of service, that are mentored in their early police careers, and align with others who share similar beliefs of integrity and justice stand the best chance of fighting against corruption in the ranks of police service.

We are likely to find some solutions from these officers when exploring current issues facing law enforcement and the communities served. It is the outliers who help point us to the problems in the police community. It is the officers who choose to follow their moral compass that demonstrate the solutions for our police culture. However, it is important to look at current history to attempt to identify any patterns that may provide additional information when exploring problems and solutions for police and marginalized communities.

Currently, one of the most important tipping points occurred August 9th, 2014 in Ferguison, Missouri. It is not my intention to question the outcome of this event. I am analyzing how it may fit in with the current issues our police communities are facing. This analysis may challenge many who read this book. However, when we can consider or entertain a thought without needing to immediately reject it, we reveal an educated mind (Aristotle). Therefore, the reader may be challenged but through consideration of the information presented, there may be answers to issues between our marginalized communities and police culture.

A white police officer and a black male interact and there is a deadly result. Regardless of public opinion, evidence presented at trial, acquittal of the police officer, or criminal history of Michael Brown, there are places where the outcome could have been different. Of course this is hindsight. However, we must always reflect on our behavior. When we look at this outcome, it is apparent that no one won. Michael Brown was shot and killed. Some have demonized Brown, saying the officer was justified to kill him. Others have viewed Brown as a completely innocent victim. Somewhere in the middle is the truth where all loss of life is tragic, the consequences reaching far beyond the dead.

Officer Wilson survived the fatal encounter with Brown. He survived the court process and was cleared of any charges. However, his life was threatened after shooting Brown by individuals outraged by his behavior. Because of the outrage from the community, he left police work.

The death of Michael Brown and the investigation, acquital, and eventual resignation of Officer Wilson illustrate the larger issue. What was going on in the police culture of Ferguson, Missouri prior to this deadly confrontation? The community members in Ferguson rioted night after night and demonstrated their anger and frustration through violence. The community demanded accountability of their police officers. Again while Officer Wilson was cleared of any charges, it does not negate the fact that the police department is still being challenged to change to this day.

Therefore, this tragic event viewed as a tipping point offers the rest of us the opportunity to examine how we could or should change our behavior in the future, both the community and the police. One year later, August 9th, 2015 in Ferguson, Missouri, police were wearing polo shirts and khakis instead of riot gear. The community reported feeling better about police, that they were getting to know them as human beings.

There is a new police chief. However, there is still rioting even though police are more reflective and more deliberate. This trend appears reactive not responsive, a quick fix instead of anatomical growth. Our ability to reflect and introspect is learning, changing, adapting, and growing. This reflection, rather than reaction, provides opportunity to change us permanently, at a neurological and cellular level.

In an investigation by the Department of Justice, it was revealed on March 4, 2015 that police officers in Fergusion Police Department did routinely violate the rights of those individuals in their marginalized communities. It was found that there was a pattern or practice of discrimination towards African Americans in the community. So regardless of the actions of both Officer Wilson or Michael Brown, the event itself demonstrated a much deeper issue within Ferguson and its police department. The community demanded change because there was a police culture in conflict with the values and goals of law enforcement; the behavior abusive rather than inclusive.

The tipping point for the city of Baltimore appears to have

occurred during the summer of 2013. In a recent article (Wallace-Wells, 2015), the author described an incident where an unarmed man was beaten by eight Baltimore police officers. His death sparked a lawsuit and investigation within the police organization. However, the city prosecutor declined to file charges on any police officer. Because the coroner ruled the death as resulting from a heart condition, there was no liability found against the officers. Nevertheless, one police leader identified that since this incident there was a feeling of something brewing beneath the surface in the city of Baltimore.

Obviously, Baltimore experienced a much larger conflict in 2015 between community and police with the death of Freddy Gray. This event clearly demonstrated that our failure to address the issues facing us in our police communities and the conflicts with community members will not go away but increase in number and intensity. Our choice to ignore what is currently happening in our police communities has become unacceptable.

Never Giving Up Ground

One of the most difficult things to realize as a police officer is our ability to create violence rather than to stop violence. Police officers are taught to maintain control; control of their emotions, control of each situation encountered, and control of people in crisis. It is very difficult to retreat when taught to advance, to take charge. The loss of control can cause a great amount of fear in a police officer. And, fear is a tremendous enemy of our higher executive functioning in our brains; that specific area in our frontal lobes where we problem solve rather than just react. However, it is imperative to remember we have the option to take a step back from these situations that are so volatile. Our ablity to think from this higher cognitive level opens up the opportunity to resolve problems more effectively.

One of the most recent examples involved a police officer in a sheriff's department in Michigan and a 17 year-old male. In February 2015, the police officer stopped the young male because the male flashed his high beam headlights at the oncoming police vehicle. The video from the police officer in contact with the young man documented the traffic contact to the tragic end where the young male screamed as he was shot by the officer.

When the young man was stopped, he told the officer that he (the law enforcement officer) had his high beams on, which was why he flashed his lights. The officer repeatedly told the youth that he did not have his high beams on, that it was a new police car, and he had stopped at least two other people for the same reason. The young man continued to be verbally defiant to the officer who appeared to remain calm. The officer also asked his communication center to send another officer to help him.

The traffic contact continued with the officer telling the young man that he needed his license, registration, and proof of insurance. The youth did not comply. The officer then told the young man that he let the other drivers off with a warning and the young man's actions were moving the contact toward a misdemeanor violation by his refusal to comply with an officer's request.

The analysis of this example left me with many quesitons. I wondered why the officer chose to pursue this contact. What was his thinking about contacting people who flashed their lights at him? Was he using this technique to find other violations through the traffic contact?

Certainly police officers are trained to look for violations beyond initial reasons for the traffic contact. Police officers are taught this behavior in their field training programs and academies. For example, a vehicle weaving in and out of a lane of traffic, the contact of the driver and vehicle, may lead to identification that the driver was driving while intoxicated.

However, this example of other drivers flashing their lights at the officer and then the officer contacting those drivers for doing so brings up many questions. Why didn't the officer stop driving the patrol car or attempt to fix the headlights? Was this an option? If the officer recognized this young man was going to continue to challenge him, why continue his own resistance? He called for back-up. Was there a reason why he had to "push" the contact? Was there no back-up available?

I am clearly aware that a 17 year-old male can injure or kill a police officer very quickly. In fact, the young male did punch the police officer in the head and did become physically assaulting. However, I am also aware that when the authority of a police officer is challenged, there can be a surge of ego in that officer. I have experienced this as a police officer and I have watched it happen with other police officers. We are given the authority to "control" the situation and when that authority is challenged, a police officer can feel personally challenged. Herein lies the problem. There can be a feeling of a loss of control, an inability to handle the situation, and a belief that we cannot give up any ground or we may be viewed as weak or ineffective.

De-Escalation

There are many times where we, as police officers, "push" the force rather than seeking de-escalation. Perhaps the officer in the previous example decided to exert more control in the contact because he "felt" he was losing control of the traffic contact and the situation went out of control, ending in a deadly result for a relatively minor offense. Whatever the circumstances, when the officer reached inside the vehicle to take control of the youth the situation spiraled out of control very quickly. The number of options available to de-escalate quickly evaporated.

Once we escalate our use of force there is usually limited time and space to stop the upward spiral of force. In watching the video of the officer and the youth, there appeared to be a time where the officer stopped talking and then reached in the car. It was in the moments of the silence where the officer could have used some type of de-escalation techniques. Again, this is hindsight. Yet, examining the situation affords learning and perhaps a better response.

However, these de-escalation techniques are not regularly taught, encouraged, or promoted in the police community. In fact, our police academies do not typically focus on this type of training. The direction of training is concentrated on the areas of high liability: use of force, deadly force, driving, etc. Yet, it is our communication skills or lack thereof that always leads us to the high liability levels of use of force.

When the youth defensively resisted the officer, he pulled away from the officer and yelled for the officer to stop grabbing him. While the young man was certainly responsible for his resistive behavior, we must understand that he was not the professional in this contact. His brain was not completely developed where he is effective at thinking rationally. His behavior at 17 years of age is typical of being defiant. And, it cost him his life. The officer pulled his Taser and shot the youth. The taser probes did not connect and was not effective in stopping the youth. Then he removed his gun and fired his weapon, killing the young male.

It is the police officer who is the professional. We are peace officers. We enforce laws and we educate people. While the single snapshot of the violent conflict between this police officer and young man may have justified the deadly use of force in this incident, the entire video of the encounter illustrated several opportunities where another direction, another path, another approach might have been used to avoid the deadly result.

When I was learning how to teach defensive tactics to police officers, I remember the instructor said, "If I put a knife and a gun on a table and ask a police officer which weapon scares him, he will always point to the knife." This is because police officers are not as familiar or as trained with a knife. The gun is familiar as police officers are highly trained with their firearm.

I believe that today you could place a gun, a knife, and a human brain (representing communication and higher levels of thinking) on the same table and almost all police officers would point to the brain because they have not had appropriate training in communication, in conflict resolution, in de-escalation, and connection with community. Those skills are unfamiliar and scary. They have not had appropriate training in integrity and professionalism on the streets.

These communication skills, either having never been acquired or taught years ago, are becoming nonexistent in our police communities. For example, California Peace Officer Standards and Training (P.O.S.T.) requires **zero** hours of communication training for law enforcement officers. In the state of New York, their police officer standards require **four** hours of training in communication skills. In the United States, there are specific and unique requirements or "standards of training" for each state, and the police agencies within those states. With over 18,000 police agencies in the United States, the emphasis on training is usually on lethal force, as this area is most litigious. Yet, there appears to be limited or no training in areas where our police officers must be skilled: Communication, Ethics, De-escalation techniques, Stress Response in Communication. Each of these areas are powerful in protecting our police officers and citizens. All of these areas precede deadly force encounters in law enforcement.

We, as a society, demand that our law enforcement officers be professional, courageous, vigilant, and self-controlled. Powers (2004), a clinical psychologist and retired commander from Chicago Police Department, lectures about this very topic. He stated, "When a police officer runs away from the gunfight or runs from danger, society declares that normalcy, and we, as a profession, declare that officer unfit for duty." So, we demand that our police officers be fearless and run toward danger. We insist that, after a police officer fights for his or her life in the street and wins, the officer will then protect his or her attacker from harm once restrained (Smith & Charles, 2010).

Yes, we are human beings and capable of mistakes. However, as professionals we must remember we are "given" our authority and our power by the people we serve. We are entrusted with that power. Our society is exponentially changing and our police departments and employees must as well. This requires that police organizations and their employees change with society and evaluate their behavior.

<u>*Questions to consider in De-escalation:*</u>

1. *Can I step back from the potentially violent situation and re-assess?*
2. *Have I explored the concept of "Preclusion" where I have exhausted all levels of control or force prior to the use of deadly force?*
3. *What are my thoughts and emotions surrounding my ability to apologize?*
4. *What other alternatives can I explore rather than physical control?*

CHAPTER 3

Social Psychology & a Culture of Evil

"Competition for external power lies at the heart of all violence."
Gary Zukav

There are certain characteristics, behaviors, and genetic codes that can exacerbate our contact with other community members and help to feed, encourage, and/or create violence among individuals. A quote from a psychiatric nurse working in The Asylum in London to a newly hired nurse was "don't you know, when you live around shit, you become shit." In April 12, 2015 Baltimore Police Department police officers arrested Freddy Gray, an African American. He was transported in a police van after his arrest, completely unrestrained. He collapsed inside the van, falling into a coma, and died on April 19, 2015 of a spinal cord injury. Very quickly a medical investigation found that he was injured during transport and his death was ruled a homicide. On May 1, 2015, the State Attorney's office filed charges on six Baltimore police officers.

Just weeks (July 2015) after the death of Freddy Gray, there was a sign found in one of the police transport vans stating, "Enjoy your ride cuz we will." There is something significantly wrong in a police culture when a sign is posted inside a police van just weeks after the injury and resulting death of an individual in a similar van. The Baltimore Police Chief was fired shortly after these events.

On April 4, 2015, Officer Michael Stager from North Charleston, South Carolina stopped Walter Scott for a non-functioning brake light. At some point during the traffic contact, Mr. Scott ran from Officer Stager, who shot Scott in the back killing him. Officer Stager claimed Mr. Scott tried to take his Taser. A witness observing the traffic contact used his cell phone to record the incident, detailing inconsistencies in Officer Stager's version. In the video, after Officer Stager shot Scott, he walked over and reached down to pick up an item, then drop that item near the body of Walter Scott. Officer Stager was charged with murder soon after the video was given to the police adminstration and district attorney.

On July 17, 2014, New York officers contacted Eric Garner. According to reports, Garner was selling single cigarettes. The contact with Eric Garner was intended to stop larger crime by attacking petty crime. He was known by police for this petty criminal behavior. In another cell phone video, the viewer can see there are several plainclothes officers around Garner. Garner's hands were visible. He was a very large individual, which may explain the number of police officers surrounding Garner.

When officers attempted to grab him and gain control, Garner struggled and attempted to pull away. The video showed an officer using a "choke hold" on Garner as he is taken to the ground. Eric Garner told officers repeatedly that he could not breathe. Officers continued to struggle with Garner, who then lost consciousness and died. There were no apparent efforts to resuscitate him.

In December 2014, a grand jury decided not to indict any officers in the death of Eric Garner. The public responded with many demonstrations against police brutality. In July 2015, New York City settled out of court and paid the Garner family $5.9 million dollars. While Garner's death may not have risen to criminal charges for the officers involved, a civil court ruled that the officers, thereby the city, were responsible for his death. And, the taxpayers shouldered the burden of the settlement.

October 2015, I attended an event at a community college in

Modesto, California. During the event, the film *Black in American: Black and Blue* (CNN, 2015) was shown as part of the program. The video began with NYPD contacting Eric Garner and then followed with thoughts and comments from NYPD officers and community members about the issues and tension between police and community. Police commissioner Bill Bratton also described his philosophy of policing, some of the mistakes made by NYPD, and what the police department is doing today to improve their community relations and police performance.

One of the most interesting points identified by community members and the police in New York is the concept of deployment of the newest police officers on the police force. Commissioner Bratton described that rookie police officers were placed in high crime areas to "attack" that crime, similar to military troops sent to "surge into enemy territory" during combat on the front lines. Unfortunately, these rookies did not know the job of police work and made numerous mistakes. The community members agreed with Bratton's perspective that this was an error in deployment, stating that it is so important to the community members to get to know them. When officers are placed in a section or district without any understanding of the location, there is ample room for mistakes, misunderstanding, and potential frustration and violence.

NYPD also identified that the majority of mistakes made by officers were being made by officers with very little experience on the street. Michael Dowd (2015) also described the importance of how an officer learns the job of police work. He said the learning from the street is very powerful. An officer will learn from his peers but will also learn from the street, "identifying the walk of someone with a gun or the sideways glance of someone who may be carrying drugs."

One of the solutions NYPD recognized was to implement supervisors spending more time with these new officers. While the concept of mentoring will be addressed in later chapters, it is important to mention the power of having police officers with years of experience, particularly supervisors, around new officers just getting started. If that new officer has no one to ask questions, correct behavior, and offer support and guidance then he or she will make up ways to survive in the environment. That may be dangerous for the new officer and the community as the new officer attempts to find solutions to problems encountered without any direction.

Commissioner Bratton talked about the belief around the "broken windows theory" still being a viable concept in policing today. This theory (Wilson & Kelling, 1982) discussed the importance of addressing disrepair in a neighborhood. When windows are broken and left unattended, there is opportunity for vandals to further the destruction. Additionally, apathy grows in the neighborhood, as the behavior signals an "uncaring" for property and the neighborhood.

However, New York Police Department then branched into a program called CompStat (Computer Statistics). It is another type of management style where there is a focus on accountability in areas experiencing high levels of crime. One anonymous NYPD officer described his belief around the concept of CompStat. He said "everything is numbers based" (CNN, 2015). He continued, stating that typically a commander is in charge of a bureau or sector or district. When something happens within that assigned area, the commander must be accountable for the crime numbers. That accountability filters down to the street officer, who is made to issue summonses or take enforcement action. This anonymous officer said "summonses must be written." His belief is the theory is wrong when it abuses and hurts the people it's suppose to protect. The officer ended by saying, "All we do is hunt them."

To date - November 2015, while I write this chapter there is one more example of a tragic, questionable police shooting. Two Louisiana police officers were charged with second degree murder after shooting and killing a six year old autistic boy. The officers contacted a truck on a traffic stop. At some point during the contact, there was a short chase, involving the truck and its occupants, and both officers fired at the vehicle, the driver, and occupants. The six year-old boy was strapped in a car seat next to his father. The boy was killed and his father, who was driving, was critically injured in the crossfire. These police officers shot at the truck and its occupants 18 times. The boy was struck in the head and chest six times and died instantly.

The event was captured on the body cameras of the officers. In several new releases, Louisiana State Police Superintendent, Mike Edmonson, described the event as very disturbing from his perspective as a father and a police officer. Initial information revealed there may have been a possible connection between one of the arrested officers and the father driving the truck, which could have led to the shooting. However, the actions illustrate a much larger picture of evil, which may simmer under the surface in many of our police communities.

Social psychological effects in policing

It is important to examine our police officers and the conflict with community from a social psychology perspective. Social psychology focuses on how individuals are influenced by society, groups, and institutions and then how that influence affects their behavior and thought processes. To my knowledge, the police culture has never been explored from this perspective.

One of the most fascinating studies in social psychology was conducted in 1971 by psychologist, Dr. Philip Zimbardo. It was the Stanford Prison Experiment and involved several college students who were solicited to participate in an experiment where they were randomly assigned to role play guards or prisoners in a mock prison. The experiment was designed to continue for two weeks. However, Zimbardo had to end the experiment after the first week when he observed very disturbing behavior in the participants, with at least three students suffering severe emotional disturbances and breakdowns. The experiment and its results are so powerful because it provides a rich understanding about how quickly the individual can be influenced and changed by the environment, situation, or culture.

Because of his research, Zimbardo has been solicited by many individuals and groups on his expertise in group dynamics as well as individual and dispositional factors influencing behavior. He has researched many situations where individuals demonstrated significant immoral or corrupt behavior, to include the prisoner abuses in Abu Ghraib. Zimbardo (2007) described the events reported in Abu Ghraib were so familiar to his 1971 experiment as they "were mirrored in real guards and real prison in Iraq of 2003." The results of both were disturbing. Yet, they provide some of the most powerful illustrations concerning our behavior in the situation rather than a "dispositional factor." So why is this important and what is the difference between the situation and the disposition?

When we attribute behavior to "dispositional factors," we are assigning behavioral characteristics to the individual. For example, we could describe the police officers who have been arrested and charged with crimes for the violence inflicted on community members as "bad apples" or "evil." This is considered "dispositional" or individual behavior. The problem is we are not considering the importance of the situation and its affect on the individual.

Exploring the same example using "situational factors," we can look at how the situation or the system affected those police officers and their behavior. This can help us explain how background checks and psychological tests failed to weed out these "bad apples." The situation places a powerful influence on the individual and we often fail to acknowledge this, either through an unawareness of the concept or by choosing to ignore it. When we choose to acknowledge the power of the situation or the system, then we must look at how that situation or system helps create the change in the individual's behavior and evaluate whether the system needs to be changed. This demands accountability and responsibility of everyone involved.

There are many tremendous examples of the power of the situation and its social influence on the individual. Hitler's regime is a perfect illustration. How could ordinary men and women commit such atrocities to the Jewish population? Were each of those individuals involved with Hitler simply evil or did the situation help create the pressure to conform to that evil?

Another example is the prisoner abuse at Abu Ghraib in 2003. These American soldiers changed their behavior very quickly and began to abuse their prisoners, taking photographs of their abusive behavior. Many of us may choose to simply say these soldiers were simply "evil." However, does it make sense that all of these soldiers who committed these terrible acts happened to meet at the same location? Or does it make more sense that the culture or environment created opportunity for this behavior to occur?

An additional illustration is the massive corruption in our correctional systems, such as the Clinton Correctional Facility in New York. In June 2015, two prisoners escaped with the help of one of the staff members at this correctional facility. However, the prison was reportedly violent to many of the prisoners and corruption was prominent. Each of these examples are reflective of the necessity to look at how our systems and organizations affect those individuals inside the systems.

Perhaps one of the reasons we do not look at systemic reasons for bad behavior is due to how quickly that behavior can change. Zimbardo (2008) shared his concerns about his own behavior when watching the participants in the Stanford Prison Experiment. His role was to monitor the participants for erratic behavior as well as participate as the "warden" or ultimate authority figure in the experiment. His belief and that of the participants was how easy it became to get lost in the role they were playing. If the behavior is changing quickly and the leaders of the organization are not cognizant of the members' behavior then the culture could change quickly and quietly, almost unnoticed until that behavior then clashes with its community.

Dispositional vs. Situational Attribution Theory

Situation attribution theory helps us explore the systemic issues in an organization or community rather than focusing on dispositional factors in the individual. Exploring our police communities from this theory is very contentious. One of the main reasons it is troublesome is we must then look at our organizations and cultures to determine how they have influenced our members. It requires our police leaders and police executives to look at how their own behavior may affect the group, the culture, and their employees. It demands accountability of all members in the organization.

If we determine that a person's behavior is the result of some individual trait or characteristic then we can assume that the bad behavior is "dispositional" or caused by some internal characteristic; or their disposition was the cause of the behavior. However, if we conclude that the behavior of an individual is influenced by the situation or environment then we have made a "situational" attribution; or attributed a behavior of the individual to the situation.

Typically when a police officer commits some type of unethical or corrupt behavior, that behavior is usually identified as a dispositional behavior; that the individual is just a bad apple that slipped through the investigatory process of a police background check. This type of attribution becomes troublesome when groups of individuals in the organization engage in corrupt behavior. How do we then explain the entire group of bad apples finding each other and managing to manipulate the screening process of police testing?

From my own experiences in police work, I often found it troubling that a police officer or a group of police officers engaged in corrupt or illegal behavior. Many times those officers were very good police officers and I would have never have believed they would have participated in any inappropriate behavior. I had never thought about how or why we attribute unethical or corrupt behavior.

For example, I remember one young police officer that excelled in the field-training program. He became a solid and dependable police officer. He then began to train other police officers. He was an informal leader on his team. He was charismatic with a great sense of humor. He displayed great decision and problem solving skills. However, he experienced a significant critical event in his life and his behavior began to change. In addition, there were substantial changes in the police organization that directly affected him and the other police officers on the team. Subsequently, he along with other police officers began to slip into some questionable and unethical behavior on duty.

In this example, a dispositional attribution of his behavior would illustrate that he must have been an unethical person before he became a police officer. He could have manipulated the testing process and managed to slip through the strict background check. However, perhaps it is necessary to think about how the situation or environment contributed to his behavior. The significant changes in the police organization and the major personal crisis in his life may have created an opportunity for him to make very poor choices. While the individual is always in choice as to how he or she will respond, we must be cognizant of the power of the situation.

We may question whether the system or organization provided an opportunity to be corrupt, such as the lack of supervision. Also, did the leaders within the system fail to identify an employee in crisis? Finally, police leaders must be aware of fostering an environment of care and concern. We can choose not to create positive and nurturing environments and then experience; burnout, job dissatisfaction, increased sick usage, high turnover, and lower discretionary employee energy (just doing the work because they love to do it).

If we explore current issues of violence and conflict in our police communities, it is important to examine how the situation, environment, or culture may be contributing to the employee's behavior. In Ferguson, Missouri, the Department of Justice found that the police community was excessively punitive towards marginalized communities members. This is an excellent example of situational attribution. The culture of the organization actually changes the behavior of the individual. The individual usually is heavily influenced to follow the social norms of the group in order to maintain their position in the group. If the individual does not follow the group norms, then he or she may suffer consequences. So a "good" police officer may choose bad behavior in order to maintain group cohesion. Those consequences of not conforming may be social isolation, loss of protection, or removal from the group. There is considerable power in the situation or environment to conform.

Therefore, our ability to explore police behavior from a situational attribution is influential if we hope to understand how our police cultures influence their members. First, understanding that our police officers that choose to commit unethical or corrupt behavior may not be bad apples but rather conforming to organizational or cultural norms helps us recognize that our selection processes may not be completely flawed. Second, it is imperative that our police leaders understand how the culture in the police organization may contribute to corrupt behavior.

For example, there is a significantly high level of corruption among correctional officers as reported by news media and correctional officers themselves. That statement does not imply that all correctional officers are bad and the selection process is completely defective. Perhaps what it does say is that there may be a culture within the correctional community that lends itself to corrupt, unethical, or illegal behavior. So our exploration into why this occurs would be to examine how the situation or environment may enhance this type of opportunity. Is the pay scale appropriate for correctional officers? Are there sufficient levels of leadership to help mentor young correctional officers? What support mechanisms are there to help correctional officers with stressors encountered in their work? Those questions may provide direction to leaders as to how the system is influencing employee behavior.

An illustration of what may happen when the culture is ignored occurred at the Clinton Correctional Facility in June 2015. Two inmates escaped with the help of one of the prison staff. The woman directly responsible for helping the inmates escape was arrested and charged. However, were there any correctional leaders or administrators within the prison system that were held accountable? Here is an excellent opportunity for leaders in this community and culture to examine how correctional staff are hired, trained, disciplined, and supported.

In another example, the Superintendent of the Chicago Police Department was asked to resign December 2015. The police video released of the shooting of a 17 year-old male in 2014 sparked a loud outcry from the public about how the Chicago Police Department handled the internal investigation. The Chicago mayor decided to ask for his resignation due to a lack of public trust in the police organization. This demonstration of forced accountability of our police leaders is powerful but necessary. Our police leaders must be held accountable for the police organizational behavior. Otherwise, the group and its behavior are not motivated to change. While the superintendent is not directly linked to the shooting death of the teenager, he is responsible for the culture that may allow or encourage corrupt or illegal behavior. That level of accountability in our police communities provides opportunity to foster ethical conduct that flows through the organization and discourages chances for corruption.

Aggression

It is important to explore aggression in our police communities from a social psychological perspective in order to examine what is happening with these horrific examples of criminal behavior. Again, the previous examples are abhorrent and are on the end of the spectrum of police behavior in our country. However, it is important to look at the behavior because it has become pronounced and has been repeated, demanding attention.

According to the National Institute of Justice website, the actual frequency of excessive force in the police community is difficult to determine (Alpert & Dunham, 2004). Currently, there is a call for better reporting regarding law enforcement use of force. Our police culture has been a very closed community. Police officers must rely on each other and there are times when the reliance is dysfunctional. Additionally, the secrecy of the culture does not afford researchers the opportunity to explore what is or is not working in the police community. For example, when researching use of force complaints it is not clear whether community members do not feel safe in reporting excessive force or whether there other reasons yet undefined that lead to the difficulty in estimating frequency of use of force. When I was conducting research in the police community in the early 2000's, I had difficulty getting officers to participate in my research until they realized I was from the police community.

In examining aggression as one of the social psychological perspectives in the police culture, we should define what "aggression" means. It may describe a range of behaviors, which may include insults to murder. But the importance of the definition lies in that aggression is behavior and not the emotions behind the behavior. The emotion may prompt the aggression. Finally, aggression is intended to hurt another person.

There are two types of aggression. There is indirect aggression, which is not face-to-face conflict. An example of indirect aggression would be gossiping about another individual, spreading rumors, or cyber-bullying. Direct aggression is face-to-face conflict, which may include attempting to physically harm someone, threatening a person, or directly insulting the individual.

If we examine aggressive behavior in police work, we should acknowledge that police officers are taught to enforce laws. A large component of enforcement requires control of individuals and situations, which lends itself to aggression but not necessarily emotion. Nevertheless, emotions can promote the aggression. The major reason of aggression in police work is the protection of oneself or members of one's group or of the communities served. It functions as a control mechanism of the situation. Police work demands that police officers maintain control, that they find order out of chaos, which lends itself to using aggression in order to accomplish that control.

However, aggressive behavior in the police culture may also occur when there is frustration. Social psychologists have identified that aggression may serve some type of function. That function may be a coping mechanism to address the frustration by acting out in an aggressive manner. If we have police communities that are stressed, overworked, under appreciated, and frustrated, we can assume that the behavioral response would be aggression.

Throughout my research in police communities in the United States and the United Kingdom as well as my own experiences as a police officer, I know there are tremendous pressures placed on police officers today. There are shortages of police officers working the streets, which creates stress and pressure to answer calls for service. Police officers in many agencies have reported having several calls waiting when they start their shift. For example, an officer may have up to 20 calls holding at the beginning of work. Working in this environment day after day increases officer stress and fatigue as well as decreases the officer's ability to recover and maintain resiliency.

There are police officers working sick or injured. Some police officers are off using sick time, creating a time burden for their peers who are left to work additional shifts. In a survey in the United Kingdom of 350 respondents, police officer/constables were asked to describe their stress levels and the effects of the stress in their work. Based on findings in the survey, the costs of stress, PTSD and Burnout in UK forces is £99 million or $152 million (Liddell, 2013).

The results of the survey in the UK could be easily be replicated in the United States. This distress in our police communities occurs here as well. Unfortunately, to date there has not been a similar study in the United States. However, in my research with police officers there was a great amount of anecdotal information that reflected similar findings of the tremendous effects of stress on police officers and their health. So, the aggressive behavior of police communities may be reflecting a much larger issue brewing underneath the surface of police organizations and systems.

The increase of frustration within the police communities may underlie a significant increase in aggression. Any unpleasant feelings or negative feelings may fuel this aggression. As police officers incur more demands from the organization, the community, and others there may be a chronic irritability that leads to aggressive behavior in order to ameliorate these feelings of frustration. As police encounter marginalized and frustrated communities, the frustration increases in themselves as well, creating a perfect storm of aggression.

Additionally from a social learning perspective in social psychology, there are times when the aggressive behavior is rewarded. There are those police officers who are celebrated for their "warrior status" and ability to fight. This behavior usually provides a poor example for impressionable new police recruits, that the behavior presented is more appropriate than what they may have learned in an academy. Oftentimes, police officers are admired for being fighters or aggressive. Many police officers seek to emulate the behavior. Finally as human beings, we are somewhat mimmicks of behavior. So violence and aggression begets violence and aggression.

Aggressive behavior is a significant a part of our genetic makeup. We are somewhat "hard wired" for aggression, anger and fear in our mid brain or "mammalian brain." It is our survival mechanism for adaptation. Those who could fight and survive had more social status because this behavior would guarantee survival of the species. Unfortunately, this type of behavior is completely inappropriate in our police force when contacting our community members under normal cirumstances. Certainly aggressive behavior is appropriate when encountering a threat or in pursuit of protecting self or others. However, the constant level of aggression in our police officers creates similar levels of aggression and frustration in our communities, almost as if our police officers become a contagion of aggression.

Sometimes aggressive police action may cause an individual or an incident to spiral out of control. Whether the behavior is caused from a high level of frustration or a need for maintaining social status, such as a warrior status, the aggression overtakes any higher level thought process in the police officer. That police officer is no longer "thinking" through the actions he or she is about to take. Instead, the action becomes a reaction rather than a response to the situation. There is no more opportunity to rationally think through the situation, to stop and evaluate consequences, or to step back and find another path. The result becomes winning the conflict at any cost.

Additionally, aggression in the police culture may be triggered by other factors beyond frustration. Usually in cultures where citizens view the laws as weak and believe they must protect themselves, violence may become a necessary response. The threat or perceived threat to a person or the culture demands retaliation, otherwise the individual or the culture may be viewed as vulnerable or an easy target. Typically, this behavior is called a "culture of honor," where the reaction to an insult or threat is aggression.

Perhaps the aggression in our police culture can be examined from the perspective of a "culture of honor" in that the perception of our criminal justice system may appear weak and the "culture" must protect itself. The members of the culture may feel unappreciated and culture then must defend against any perceived threat. Any challenge or action against what the culture has determined is right or lawful must be met with aggression. Rather than the enforcement of laws, it becomes the defense of the honor of the culture.

The loss of higher levels of thinking or problem-solving then generates a loss of fluidity or flexibility in the response of the officer. At this point, the officer can only hope that he has the advantage in the fight and can "win" the encounter. Because, in this situation only one combatant wins. However, if the goal of the confrontation is to achieve a higher understanding, or to educate the individual, then all parties in the confrontation can succeed. We must learn to "think" with the prefrontal cortex of our brain and respond appropriately rather than simply react aggressively.

Prejudice and Implicit Bias

One of the most difficult topics to discuss is the subject of prejudice or biases, particularly in today's culture of anger and fear surrounding marginalized communities, racism, and inequality. Most individuals do not want to admit that they have biases or prejudices that may influence how they respond in certain situations. When teaching psychology courses, I usually have my students take the *Implicit Association Test*, (2011) which requires them to take a test about how they respond to implicit associations about race, gender, sexual orientation, or other sensitive topics.

Invariably, I have several students who get angry because they believe the test implied that they showed a preference to one race over another and that meant they were prejudiced. The exercise provides a great opportunity to explain the power and importance of "implicit bias," which are those biases that we are not even aware of, those biases that lurk beneath the surface of our behavior, influencing our behavior. These biases are subtle cognitive processes that operate below conscious awareness and may cause conflict with behavior and belief in the individual. The exercise is powerful for students because then they understand that their behavior can be influenced by beliefs and familiarities that they were completely unaware of until taking the test. The knowledge of implicit bias also provides the students the ability to understand their behavior and the chance to change their behavior if they so choose.

Yet, we all have prejudices and biases. We all stereotype and categorize the world around us. It is a necessity in order to organize our world where there are over seven billion people. What becomes dangerous or dysfunctional is when we do not know what our biases are or we are unwilling to look at our behavior in order to change. In an interview with a white male police officer in one of the southern states, he stated he was assigned to a section of the city where there were a majority of African Americans. He said initially his behavior toward the community was "typical" in that he believed many were "criminals." He had randomly assigned this characterization to a group of people without any higher-level thinking. He made a huge assumption based from his beliefs. However, he then started to "anchor" himself mentally into understanding what he described as the "community of color." He said his attitude toward the community changed to compassion rather than being frustrated with the community once he could understand where each of these individuals were coming from with their own experiences.

His coping strategy for working in the community is exemplary. He recognized his biases and how those biases affected his ability to work in that section of his city. He worked to change those biases, moving toward compassion and understanding regardless of the color of skin and regardless of the type of contact.

In the video *Black in America: Black and Blue* (2015), police commissioner Bratton discussed the amount of contacts made by New York Police Department, particularly with the African American communities. According to their statistics, there have been over 5 million stops or contacts. The concept of "stop and frisk" is still very controversial. There have been many police mistakes made using this concept, such as illegal detention. Some community members report having been stopped by police over a hundred times.

Commissioner Bratton stated the number of stops or contacts should be declining when crime goes down. New York City has experienced a decrease in crime for the last two years. In fact, in 2013 New York City experienced 24 hours without any criminal activity (LexisNexis, 2013). Yet, the numbers for contacts remain enormously high and have created a deterioration of trust between police and its citizens. This behavior illustrates the absolute need for systemic changes in our police organizations and how biases, prejudices, and stereotypes influence police culture.

To change an individual's belief about previously held prejudicial or biased based beliefs requires higher cognitive thought processes. Individuals must engage in wanting to change and open their perspectives and belief systems. They must be willing to expose themselves to people that may challenge those previously held beliefs. The individual must attempt to get to know the "other." This requires individuals to be introspective and inquisitive. It demands that they shed those limiting beliefs and open themselves to new experiences that reinforce new beliefs.

Failure to assimilate higher thought patterns and non-limiting beliefs around different ethnicities or types of people only fosters separation, anger, and fear. When we choose to identify others as less than ourselves, we become "justified" to treat them differently or "less than." Our tendency to separate ourselves in the police community creates the "us versus them" mentality that has a tremendous effect on police officers.

Police officers often fall into the mentality of "us versus them," which affords them the opportunity to separate from community, family, friends, and eventually anyone who is not a police officer. With that isolation comes a strong need to defend and close ranks, to protect that group no matter what.

Groups

Many have described the profession of law enforcement as the largest gang in the United States. This is an unfortunate depiction of police work. However, it is important to address the power of groups, issues of authority, and identification with groups as it affects our behavior.

In social psychology, groups are fascinating and an important area to explore as our behavior in groups has a tremendous effect on the individual. For example, groups can provide a larger sense of identity. Or a group may offer safety or belongingness, all of which are very important to human beings. We are all part of groups from the beginning of our life. It starts with our families and moves to other loved ones and friends, then work, and perhaps religion or education. Groups allow us to share a common vision.

Entering the profession of law enforcement provides a unique opportunity to belong. The police family is a strong cohesive group that fosters a sense of belonging. There is a common vision to keep the peace and protect the public. Additionally, police work tends to promote the behavior of deindividuation, or a lessening of individual identification. Police officers wear a uniform, dressing the same. Their behavior is governed by rules and procedures of the group. Each of these deindividuation behaviors causes a loss of self and a stronger identification with the police group rather than the individual.

Deindividuation in groups can create a significant problem. Individuals begin to feel anonymous but empowered to act or behave differently in a situation. In police work, this concept can be the behavior of the team or shift of officers who choose to act differently than each individual officer may act. In my own experiences as a supervisor,

I have seen very good officers choose to comply with a new norm on a patrol shift, such as violating an organizational rule and sleeping on duty, when they never would have behaved that way as an individual.

According to Zimbardo (2008), there are three components associated with deindividuation: arousal, anonymity, and lack of responsibility. If the cohesion of the group is strong, then the members are more willing to take greater risks than they would as individuals. People may commit acts that they would not normally do if they were alone. The responsibility is lessened because there is anonymity in the group. The arousal of taking chances builds the cohesiveness of the group.

In examining police culture and corruption, it is easy to understand that groups often provide police officers the capability to "hide" bad behavior within the group, team, or shift. A recent example was found in the transport van in the city of Baltimore. Just weeks after the death of Freddy Gray, a reporter found a handwritten note that stated, "We hope you enjoy your ride, cuz we will." The anonymity of the behavior is transferred among all members, without any member accepting responsibility. The group begins to make decisions based on a risky shift, whereby the responsibility for the decision is spread among its members. So decisions that an individual would find highly apprehensive when not in the group become a confident choice inside the group as responsibility is lessened.

Finally, one of the most dangerous behaviors in groups is "groupthink." The group becomes so engrossed in their decision or behavior that the members fail to look at alternative options or choices. For example, a patrol team that has become extremely cohesive chooses to engage in some type of corrupt behavior. The team begins to establish some new group norms. Perhaps the team members decide to take money from a crime scene rather than enter the money into evidence. Team members would then share the money with each member of the team, inculcating them into the new group norm of taking money illegally, maintaining secrecy, and protecting the group and its members. It becomes more important to protect the group rather than report the illegal or unethical behavior.

This group behavior fosters strong unity among its members. Should a member fail to accept the money then he or she risks social isolation, lack of protection from the group members, or separation from the group. While the group member may engage in the behavior, the motivation for the agreement may be one of fear or a strong need to belong rather than the member being evil or bad. Consequently, our police leaders and supervisory staff must be cognizant of group dynamics in order to help prevent this group behavior.

CHAPTER 4

Policing as a "Business"

*"To solve the human equation, we need to add love, subtract
hate, multiply good, divide between truth and error"*
Janet Coleman

During an early morning walk in the fall of 2015, I was thinking about reasons for our current difficulties in the police community. I remembered that sometime in the early 2000's, my police department made the decision to "move to a business plan." I was working as a community resource officer at the time and had just completed a very difficult assignment working with a community in distress due to a drug dealer living in their neighborhood. We were able to get him put in prison, evict him from his home, and bring some peace and safety back to this neighborhood. I had a great sense of accomplishment as I had closely worked with this neighborhood community for two years. Now a commander was telling me that the police department was moving to a business plan, which did not make sense and seemed to move our police organization away from a service model.

I was not the only police officer who questioned this organizational move, or perhaps did not understand. I look back and can feel the confusion today. Our police department was moving toward "decentralized policing" and a business plan. I was due to be promoted to the rank of sergeant in 2003 and was told that there would be significant changes in scheduling police officers, moving toward schedules that allowed maximum coverage over the week. Certainly, the concept of maximum coverage of police services is excellent when viewed from a business and safety perspective.

Yet, the human factor should be considered and the organization's members should know that "management" is considering how the change affects them. The schedule change was drastic and police officers with several years of seniority were now being told that they would lose the schedules that allowed them to have at least a part of the weekend off. Having part of the weekend off provided some normalcy in their lives as well as connection with family members on regular work schedules. Now they had days off in the middle of the week, disrupting family schedules, and lessening patrol morale.

This new schedule is one example of the changes that began to be implemented using a business plan. Those officers with the highest seniority benefitted from the schedule and those officers just starting out their careers really did not know what they were missing. The larger portion of our patrol division experienced the biggest changes to their schedules. Suddenly, there was an infusion of low morale because these officers were radically affected in their work schedules. These schedules affected their families, their social life away from work, and their beliefs around how the organization now viewed them. The staff began to feel unappreciated by the administration. Schedule changes were just one factor of moving toward a business model in policing.

The concept of the business plan model began around the introduction of CompStat (Computer Statistics), which is a "combination of management philosophy and organizational management tools for police departments" (Wikipedia). This was an accountability process for the New York City Police Department, designed to reduce crime and improve the quality of life. Commanders and other police executives used CompStat for personnel and resource management, using comparative statistics to address areas of high crime. The process became more important than the personnel.

My perspective is police officers became 'widgets' rather than people, the focus centering on the goals of the district or bureau and not the members in the organization who were working those beats or districts. There were subtle changes in language that reflected the organization's change. For example, shifting a goal to a ten percent reduction of criminal activity in a district or sector rather than having an organizational goal that acknowledges the people that are affected by that criminal activity has a different effect on the culture of the organization. The focus is centered on the number or percentage rather than on the human being.

In 2010, I was in London working on research in the police community. I was interviewing a police executive who told me, "You Americans, you have no idea how to police." Certainly, the cop in me was immediately insulted. However, I had to remind myself that I was interviewing him for research in the police community and it was important to get these interviews from another continent to determine if the research I was doing in the United States in the police community was relevant in another country. My injured ego was not a concern.

His comment was powerful and applicable to this problem of a shift in perspective in our police community today. When I look back at the statement, I wonder if he understood the power of those words or if he was making a quick assumption about policing in the United States. He elaborated on his words and said that the police force in the United Kingdom had already tried CompStat, that all of the programs we were currently trying in the United States had already been tried in the UK and failed. All of these computer statistical programs were not effective in his opinion and each had been discarded.

Additionally, he said he did not understand how the United States police agencies could function properly when each agency had its own rules and standards, rather than a unified force like the United Kingdom. This police leader believed it impossible to present a unified police service when the 18,000 individual police agencies in the United States were guided by their own rules and procedures rather than the national approach of police services illustrated by the United Kingdom.

He told me that the UK police community was moving toward building relationships with their communities. He said their officers/constables now go out into the community and ask members how they want to be policed. He described that their officers ask the elderly, the skateboarder, the business man how they should be policed. He said it was even important to ask the criminal this same question.

The police executive's words were recorded for my research but I also imprinted them in my concept of policing. His words rang true for me and when I went back to my agency, I remember the complete disregard from my commanders and police executives as I tried to impart the importance of his message. It was apparent we were operating in a business plan and the topic was not open for consideration. Similar to my experience of initial anger and insult from the police executive's comment, my commanders, deputy chiefs, and chief did not want to hear that there was anything wrong with how "they police."

Additionally, a business-based approach in policing can be a fear-based model, which actually creates tension and anxiety. The model promotes statistics and numbers rather than engagement in community. The police officer is not responsible for what happens in the district or area of concern. This allows an officer to disengage from his or her work as a public servant. The boots on the ground police officer is no longer in the equation of solving community problems. He or she becomes a cog in the wheel, a widget, a chess piece to be moved. The commander or police leader is responsible for meeting the goal of the sector or district and that police leader then moves those "widgets" around in order to accomplish that goal.

It is interesting to now look back on this time. I certainly understand the egocentricity that is in the United States policing model. We are a country of individuals, believing we know best, that our way is best. However, I wonder whether it may benefit us to explore an incorporation or adoption of best practices from a national police service.

In fact, some of our states have combined certain divisions, sharing costs and responsibilities with other municipalities. For example, there has been a shift with police and sheriff's departments combining communication centers, evidence divisions, and crime laboratories. The concerning issue is the potential loss of leadership within these divisions or the confusion of leadership between the combined organizations. A systemic shift is important; a change in behavior is imperative.

CompStat

The CompStat movement came from the "broken window theory" (Wilson & Kelling, 1982) where abandoned or graffiti properties are targeted by criminals, thereby generating police attention and action. However, the "broken window theory" still employs community involvement. Police officers are responsible for identifying these areas through community feedback, active patrol, and other responsive techniques. The subtle shift from this theory to CompStat is a shift to numbers and away from organizational value in its members.

The commanders or police executives assigned to a district or area are responsible to have an effect on the crime identified by the statistics. Should the commander fail to meet agency goals, he or she may be removed/fired/demoted for failure to perform. As said previously, this is a fear-based model of performance. Working in such an environment constricts creativity, promotes tension and anxiety, and creates separation, not unity.

When I began my career in law enforcement, I remember each patrol car had stenciled on the door, "to protect and serve." When I chose the policing profession, I wanted to be of service. I have discussed with many police officers the concept of "service." There have been many officers who said that they were not "public" servants and did not like the concept on the door of their police car. However, these same officers were not taught or were not familiar with the concept of a service career. Police work has been identified as a profession of service since Sir Robert Peel's implementation of the Metropolitan Police Act. We adopted these principles in our own policing style in the United States by our two main goals: To prevent crime and protect lives.

I have taught in the police community for years, field trained many police officers, and supervised different work groups in police organizations. The majority of new police officers, those who love police work, and our most sage cops have repeatedly told me that they wanted to be police officers or became a police officer in order to help people. They did not choose to be police officers to abuse people or hurt anyone. They did not crave power. They chose to serve their communities, to work long hours and see horrific scenes, and try to protect life and property.

In our business model, there is a shift in leadership within the police structure. There is a loss of leadership and an increase of management. I have witnessed this in my own career and have heard it repeatedly in my research with police officers on two separate continents. I remember one of my officers telling me one day that he would walk through fire for me. Did that make me a good leader? No, that gave me a template to work toward becoming a good leader. That gave me hope that I could become a good leader. I also told him I would walk through fire for him, for our team. Again, the example does not assume I am a police leader. That path is proven each day, each shift with men and women in the police culture. That course is the high road of truly caring for those employees that work for you, disciplining them when they fall out of line, and mentoring them to take your job.

However, our business model creates tension and anxiety. The goal shifts to "get ahead," to better oneself, to advance. Management of programs, projects, and people becomes the goal. Leadership falls away and when this goes away, the police troops are left alone without much direction or guidance. Many police officers become focused on "getting ahead" because that is encouraged. The perception is that the goal is to be promoted as quickly as possible.

Police officers used to pride themselves on becoming the best at their profession, to be a "good cop." It was not about getting ahead or getting promoted and while I do not suggest that this concept is bad, I am stating that often officers are promoted without truly understanding the position they left. Therefore, they may not be able to "lead" the men and women in patrol. Again, the shift in thought is away from our police officers and is centered on self.

There is nothing wrong with a business plan. Nor is there anything wrong with holding others accountable or defining a problem using statistics. Key concepts that do not mix well in police work using a business model: 1. The human factor and the satisfaction of the human factor in the organization and the community are usually not a priority. The priority becomes the numbers, what it takes to reduce numbers, and how to show direct results and 2. The police culture does not "produce" anything. It is not about profit or selling a product. A police organization serves the public, protects its members, and is given authority by the public to maintain order and protect lives.

In the CNN video (2015) an anonymous NYPD police officer stated, "All we do is hunt them," when describing the interaction with "people of color." He chose to remain anonymous because of fear of retribution. He also described, "Everything is numbers based." Commanders must explain why something happens in their assigned sector or district and are punished for an increase in crime. That "punishing" behavior is pushed down to the beat police officer to "fix" the increase in higher crime statistics and, therefore, contacts increase, tickets increase, enforcement increases. This anonymous police officer described that there needs to be a systemic change in policing, stating "It (the system) works if you don't look like me," (the implication being if the person is white, the system works).

Again, there is nothing wrong with the business model in police organization. The original concept of CompStat is an excellent action for accountability and focus. The problem is the interpretation by the police executives from other organizations as the plan is implemented in their own organizations and/or the belief that the model or any model will "fix" everything. It becomes diluted from the original idea of CompStat. So, while it is important to look at the effects of a business model in a police organization, this is just one possible variable affecting our police communities.

Often I am asked about how I would change this potential discord in our police organizations. First, I do not believe that is my function here. I am suggesting we look openly at the effects of how we manage our police organizations. Can we see low morale in the police officers? Are there areas of corruption or opportunities for corruption within police organizations that have been ignored? Using a business plan, can we change language to incorporate the importance of the human being working on the street, protecting and serving? Those questions may provide information leading to change for the police culture and offer alignment with the value of our employees and the service they provide.

Managing vs. Leading

The changes in police work are numerous. Having been in police work for 27 years, I have seen changes from directed patrol, community policing, problem-oriented policing, CompStat, broken-window's theory, and many other approaches. Many times police organizations shift philosophies when there is a change in leadership in the organization or perhaps when there is a community need and/or demand. Each program or direction has an effect, shift, or ripple in the police organization. However, some of the programs or concepts shift responsibility and contact with employees and community, which can result in some concerning consequences.

Police organizations identifying with a business plan change language to reflect that plan. Supervisors can become "managers" rather than sergeants or police leaders. The concept of manager is completely different than a leader. The idea of manager implies one who oversees production, movement, or function whereas a leader represents someone who guides or encourages performance.

Additionally, there can be a subtle shift in language with terms in the police function. For example, a "call for service" or an "incident" becomes a "job." While the change in language may seem inconsequential, the change is the loss of service and a shift to the burden of the job. We are often not aware of how influential our words are on our physical and mental state. There is a difference when an officer describes "several calls holding" versus a statement of "jobs stacked" in the queue. These modifications in language have an effect and the feeling of work changes.

There can be a slight shift away from what the purpose of our work is: to serve. That concept of service can shift away from police supervisors or managers and their employees. As explained earlier, in a business concept the employee becomes less important as the focus is on the goal, target, or number. The employee is just the tool to reach the goal and that shift can lead the employee to begin to identify with the lack of boundaries, the loss of authority, and the lessening of value to the organization.

This can be an indirect result of a business model of policing. There is a very subtle change in language, in re-ordering and re-prioritizing goals and objectives. Supervisors are usually not on the street with the police officer, but rather inside the building "managing" administrative tasks. The focus is removed from mentorship and nurturing the profession and the police officer. The focus is accountability. The commander of the district or sector is now accountable for the crime within that area. So the subtle shift is to address the crime rather than how do we police that area of the community, or whether our police officers are functioning well and feel confident in their work.

It is my belief that the loss of leaders within the police community and the shift towards "managing" people has affected our police community. There has been a loss of mentorship within the profession. The manager does not have the time to spend with the employee to demonstrate complexities within the profession, the competencies that give an officer inner strength and value, and compassion for the sense of service. The manager is accountable for increases and decreases in production. The leader is accountable for the soul and the mind of the police officer.

Egoic Goals

One of the most interesting lessons in my career as a police officer is the resurfacing of my own ego. Let us examine how this ego begins for a police officer. First, we have young men and women who are given the authority and public trust to take away someone's rights as well as the ultimate; someone's life. It is a heavy responsibility for such a young person.

Additionally, the human brain does not fully develop until around age 25, which could mean we have another set of potential consequences concerning police behavior. Typically, police officers enter the career in their early twenties when their frontal lobes of the brain are still under construction. This area of the brain is our higher executive functioning, our morals, our compassion, and problem solving.

So we begin with police officers that are not thinking at their optimum level and we hand them the ultimate authority. Then we tell them to act professionally, protect the public, and arrest those that violate the law. Yet, these young police officers begin to equate violating the law with those individuals who are questioning authority. Police officers can be "offended" by that questioning when they think everyone should just follow their "lawful orders."

As a young police officer, I remember my police trainer trying to teach me about "officer presence." He did not explain it very well but invited me to demonstrate that I understood the concept during a traffic contact. I stopped a young man for some minor traffic violation. I yelled at the kid to give me his driver's license and then returned to the patrol car. My police trainer explained my errors, that officer presence was how I presented myself without having to say anything. He said, "maybe you could just ask him for his license." With a better understanding, I returned the young man's documents with a calm demeanor.

Think of how confused that young man must have been or what impression I made on him that night. He had done nothing to deserve my yelling, even though he committed a traffic violation. The lesson was important for me in understanding the importance of officer presence, that I could calm a situation by presenting "peace" and compassion, strength and confidence; and, I could destroy all that with just a few words. I would have loved to apologize to that young man.

Many years later, my ego rose again. I responded to a call of a semi truck stuck in the snow in front of an elementary school. The weather conditions were very poor and dangerous. It was snowing and cold. The roads were slick and covered with ice. I needed to get that semi truck out of the road so the school buses could get to the school.

I contacted the driver, who told me he had forgotten his tire chains and was trying to turn his truck around to go back to his house and get his chains. I gave him a stern warning, telling him he was required to have chains in this weather, and he should have never left his home without the tire chains. An hour later, I was dispatched to the same location. He was now stuck in the opposite direction on the same road. I was suddenly very angry. Had he not heard anything I said before? Why did he not follow my instructions and orders?

While I yelled at him about his "stupidity," that truck driver had his cell phone out as he was talking with his employer. His employer heard my tirade and reported me to my police chief. After I finished there at the scene, the police chief called me to his office and asked me to explain my behavior. I had no explanation. He told me to find a class to "fix" my behavior "pretty d--- quick." I did as I was told and found a class. However, the immediate lesson was that I was held accountable for my actions. I had the opportunity to recognize how my ego influenced my behavior and decisions, and I had a clear understanding that this driver was not "disobeying" me, perhaps the direction I had given him. However, that is not directly tied to who I was as a police officer, as the authority I have is not attached to me personally.

This attachment to ego and a police uniform can be hurtful and harmful. I was fortunate to have been taught by others to recognize the interference of ego in the goal of police work. To see police officers become offended by insults or behavior is disturbing. The behavior of the individual does not reflect on the individual behind the badge. Yet, time and again we see police officers using disparaging language or acting aggressively when the citizen or criminal says something offensive. I remember being taught in Verbal Judo that police officers have the right to take away someone's freedom. What is the harm in letting the person say whatever they need to if we have taken their freedom and arrested them? When we then take away someone's right to say whatever he or she wants to, then we have created a dangerous situation where that person is backed against a wall with nothing to lose.

Lowering of Standards

One of the most interesting shifts I observed during my tenure in police work was the move towards lowering standards within law enforcement. I have observed police organizations where the police chief decided not to use polygraphs to check the veracity of the police applicants. That police executive decided to hire a police applicant based on "getting a good feeling" about them.

I have also worked in police organizations that chose to allow police officers to test for the rank of sergeant with less than two years on the street. To learn the profession of policing requires many years of experience. A police officer attempting to test for promotion before having significant experience on the streets and in the community is doing a tremendous disservice to himself, the organization, and the community. The organization that allows or fosters its employees to test for promotion without having significant years of experience is also doing a tremendous disservice to the community, the organization, and its employees. Unfortunately, two years is not enough time to learn how to mentor other police officers, to be prepared to discipline those officers (both positively and negatively), and manage criminal/patrol investigations and crime scenes.

It is necessary for police officers to develop skills and abilities as well as confidence through their experiences on the street and in the community. The maturation of a police officer is necessary as it helps develop trust between the police officer and their peers. They can depend on that potential supervisor to do the right thing. They believe they will be treated fairly and that the new supervisor will value their work. What I have seen from inexperienced, new supervisors is a tendency to hide from working the streets, to become "the buddy" to those on the team, and a failure to address the little behaviors that lead toward larger transgressions of unethical behavior.

So what is the solution when there are no employees that meet a set standard for promotion? The police organization must then examine how to find the next supervisor. Perhaps there should be some introspection as to why there are no viable candidates with more tenure. Senior police officers choosing not to promote may offer important insights as to why there are not any viable applicants. If the organization has no senior or tenured police officers then a reflection as to "why" applies as well. Is the police community starting over or just developing? Otherwise, there should be some tenured police officers to help with the introspection into organizational development.

Frank Serpico (2014) recently provided his opinion concerning the current issues in law enforcement. Since his departure from the New York Police Department in 1971, he does not believe that much has changed. He challenges our police organizations to strengthen their selection processes, using psychological screening for new officers. Serpico detailed the importance of ongoing training, using scenario and simulation training. He said community involvement is imperative for police officers. He stated it is important to support the "good guys" and enforce laws equally, which includes police officers. Finally, he reiterates again that the police cannot police themselves.

We run a huge risk of experiencing severe consequences when we lower our standards in hiring or promoting in our police communities. Those "quick fixes" may lead the organization toward unethical behavior or corruption. Additionally, the lowering of standards may allow individuals who are not suited to the profession of policing, which may result in tremendously negative effects for those individuals. Former LAPD Police Chief, Daryl Gates, clearly illustrates this when he said, "No police department should hire more quickly than they can assimilate the people that they bring in, and we did. I take responsibility for it" (FRONTLINE, 2001).

The shortages of police personnel should demand that we reassess reasons for the scarcity of applicants. Is the profession experiencing shortages from those retiring from the profession or are police officers leaving for other reasons? What can we learn from these shortages? There are often plenty of opportunities to learn what is occurring inside our police communities through exit interviews usually given by human resource departments within the organization. However, those exit interviews may not be as truthful as we would like because the police leaders may not wish to acknowledge what actually may be happening within the police community. The transparency of the police organization would maximize the opportunity for those leaving the police community to share their reasons for leaving.

We need not throw out the concept of the business plan in police organizations. The shift towards a "business model" may provide better ways to address crime and promote accountability. However, there are some powerful effects using this type of model in our police communities. We must find a way to reconnect with our troops and community. Rather than simply checking off the tasks we complete, we must re-engage with our employees. If they feel valued in an organization then, in theory, they will extend those feelings of value to community and service. If we choose to use a business model to run our police organization, then we should be aware of the potential consequences as well.

<u>*Business model questions*</u>
1. What is the goal of the organization?
- to reduce crime or protect human sanctity-
2. What language fosters meaning and purpose in our work?
3. What detracts from our mission in police work?

CHAPTER 5

Stress & Service

"Honest self assessment is the first step in healing"
Ernest Holmes

One of the interesting things about police officers and police work is that it remains a very closed community. There appears to be a fear or concern about becoming vulnerable to others outside of the community. Additionally, isolation is a natural result of the secrecy of police culture. Both of these variables create problems in the police community because any grouping that fosters secrecy runs the risk of increasing dysfunctional behavior. The result is we just do not have a clear picture of what is working or not working in the police community.

Police officers are trained and disciplined to maintain control and find order out of chaos. However, the continual confrontation of human destructiveness and suffering can take a toll on police officers. Police officers are taught and tend to compartmentalize these significant, critical calls. These experiences can build up inside the police officer and increase his or her chances of undisclosed trauma, depression, anxiety, PTSD, or other physiological disorders, such as high blood pressure, obesity, and heart disease. Additionally, the inability to process crises can lead an officer to anger and dysfunctional thinking.

For example, one recent case in the news involved a police officer attempting to control a group of juveniles who were involved in
some type of altercation at a school. The juveniles were unarmed but
would not comply with the officer's orders. That officer acted very
aggressively as he attempted to control one of the juveniles. He was
immediately disciplined in light of the current issues between police
and marginalized communities. However, the police officer described
that before responding to the juvenile altercation, he had been called
to a death of an infant. He said that he was traumatized by the prior
call, which affected his behavior at the next call. This type of call can
seriously affect an officer. Yet, we do not focus on educating our police
officers on self-care techniques or problem-focused coping skills.

We demand that our police officers are professional, displaying
high integrity and moral judgment. Yet, many police officers are subjected to call after call of devastation and evil. Many times the officer
is not afforded any opportunity to process the trauma of the previous
call. Many of our police executives have not provided the atmosphere
by which police officers can relieve the stress of the previous calls
for service. Much of this may be due to increased calls for service,
decreases in police staffing, and the general disregard for the health
and welfare of police employees.

Police officers may find themselves responding to a violent situation, such as the death of a baby where the mother's boyfriend
has struck the baby's head against the wall to "shut it up." As soon
as that call is complete, the officer may go to a traffic accident or a
minor neighborhood dispute where neighbors are arguing about a
dog barking. The police officer has not had any time to process emotions surrounding the death of the baby but is expected to handle this
minor dispute with professionalism and compassion. There is anger
and frustration from the prior call and irritation about the pettiness
of the second call. Perhaps the officer has skipped a meal to problem
solve another homeless person trespassing at a local business. Then
there is that one person who challenges that officer and is confronta-
tional. Each separate incident can take its toll on that police officer.

The individual who has challenged the officer does not know what has happened before being contacted. The resulting clash between the officer and the community member can be volatile, even deadly.

Our police officers are human beings who have chosen to work in a profession that requires a high level of composure when confronting evil and human destructiveness. When we fail to care for our police officers, we set up the scenario previously described. The behavior is not an excuse. The violence perpetrated on another where it is not warranted is not acceptable and officers must be held accountable.

However, our police organizations, police leaders, and police officers must be aware that there are repercussions from the traumatic experiences encountered in the daily work of a police officer. We cannot simply assume that police officers are unaffected by their work because they fail to tell anyone. It is incumbent for our police leaders to value their police officers. We must explore the fitness of our police officers as they engage in some of the most stressful work. In this chapter, we will examine some of the research on stress and the effects on the human body, illness and health, and wellbeing in the police profession. What can we do to help our police officers not just survive but thrive in their work?

Research within the police culture is difficult as there is still a significant code of silence (Violanti, 1999). There is a general distrust from "outsiders;" anyone who is not in the police culture. There are vast responsibilities in police work and it is completely unacceptable to show any weakness to the public (Violanti, 1999; Waters & Ussery, 2007; Charles, 2009). However, there are many examples of police officers who are healthy, functioning well, and engaged in community. These police officers were the focus of my research and they offer many solutions to the issues we are now seeing between police and marginalized communities.

When I interviewed police officers across the United States and in the United Kingdom, one of the questions asked was how they coped with human destructiveness and suffering. Many of the officers shared that they understood it was their job to handle the trauma and pain. Most police officers understood that their involvement in these stressful incidents was part of a larger picture that they may not agree with or understand, that their service was like a tool of justice. Some described their police work as the "Karma Police" or an "implement of God" (Charles, 2009).

The perception of these police officers was important to identify in this research. Their ability to change their perspective of the trauma and move the experience away from a negative perception provides these officers with the ability to cope with the stressor encountered. Instead of the experience viewed as threatening or debilitating, the encounter becomes a challenge with a potential for growth.

Those police officers who are ill-prepared, experiencing overwhelming stress, or unable to identify resources to help in the situation will suffer a significant stress response. The physiological responses to that police officer are impactful. Heart rate increases, blood vessels constrict, and cognitive abilities are affected when that officer confronts extreme stress or trauma. If that stress exceeds the officer's optimal level of performance then that stress is no longer considered positive but rather a negative response on health and wellbeing. The stress becomes "distress," which can lead to "dis-ease" in the mental and physical health of the police officer.

As the stress accumulates in the body, the effects can be harmful. Chemicals are released, such as cortisol (a stress hormone), which can lead to increases in fatty tissue and weakening of the immune system. Heart rates increase and remain high as blood vessels remain constricted, which may lead to high blood pressure. Adrenalin is released during each stressful event that the police officer confronts, which may lead to enlargement of the adrenal glands.

Some coping mechanisms also perpetuate the harmful effects of stress. For example, many police officers stop engaging in healthy options. A lack of exercise, eating unhealthy or highly processed foods, consuming alcohol excessively, and smoking are many of the paths of ineffective coping often chosen by police officers under stress.

Should this overexposure to stress or trauma continue over a long period of time, the physical body begins to experience a stage of exhaustion. During the exhaustion phase of the stress response, the body is no longer able to adapt to the stress encountered. Resistance to the stressors weakens and energy is depleted. The physical body experiences a breakdown where illness and disease take their toll on the police officer. Currently the average death rate of police officers is usually ten to fifteen years earlier than the rest of the population (Violanti, 1999).

The stress responses illustrated in the preceding paragraphs are typical of all human beings who are under stress. Police work is a tremendously stressful profession. Therefore, our police officers must be prepared for how their work may affect them and their health. The physical dangers encountered, ineffective court systems, organizational conflicts, and increasing conflicts between the community and police all add significantly to the stress in police work. Additionally, we do not do a good job in educating our police officers about the effects of stress and their health. We do not illustrate that the choices our police officers make are powerful and provide rich resources for them to move their negative experiences into positive growth.

Those police officers I have interviewed on two separate continents were able to articulate how their faith in something "larger than self" afforded them the ability to encounter the daily stressors in police work positively (Charles, 2009, Charles, et al., 2014). That did not mean that they were unaffected by the human destructiveness and suffering they confronted. But rather, they were able to recognize their stress responses to the event, observe the incident as a challenge, and then act to resolve the challenge using all their available resources. Because of their capability to respond to the stressor in this manner, the effects of the stress were minimized.

When we look at the importance of teaching our police officers how to respond to stress, I am often reminded of how I was trained, how others were trained, and the continuing failure to train our police officers in the stress response. For example, I have written previously about the New York Police Deparment's "surge" deployment as described by Police Commissioner Bratton. Using a similar military approach, they deployed their newest and youngest police officers into the high crime areas of New York City.

These new police officers did not know the job, nor did they understand what the effects of not understanding the job were. Community members did not trust them. There were mistakes made by the rookies. Those mistakes have consequences beyond the obvious legal and procedural mistakes. Other consequences are the stress effects on the individual police officer.

In my training as a new police officer, there was no information on how police work may affect me. During my second day as a police officer, my sergeant assigned me to go and observe an autopsy that was being done on a young female who died from a heroin overdose. The reason for that assignment was to see if I could "handle" the stress of seeing a dead body. I had previous family experience with death and that experience was not traumatic for me. Unfortunately, I was "used" to seeing death. Additionally, my sense of commitment to learning as much as I possibly could about police work allowed me the ability to view this stressor as positive rather than negative. I knew that this type of experience came with the job.

However, none of my first trainers ever thought to discuss what occurs when an individual is under stress. My belief is they had not been taught about the effects of stress as well and, therefore, they could not teach what they did not know. Consequently, it is imperative that we begin to teach police officers about the physiological effects of stress on their health. This can help create healthy police officers that are better prepared to take care of themselves.

Police officers typically enter police work to "help;" to do something meaningful with their lives. When an officer encounters human destructiveness and suffering beyond any understanding and then confronts a community that fears and distrusts that police officer, there is a chronic level of stress that he or she now faces. It is very easy to look at this example and understand how a young police officer may go astray when left to his or her own to figure out how to serve a city of eight million people, many of whom do not like them. Certainly, this type of training, or lack there of, has a tremendous effect on a new police officer.

The loss of meaning and purpose in the profession can creep into the police officer's perspective when feeling undervalued by the organization and the community members. As the officer exerts a sense of service, experiences dissatisfaction with job accomplishments, and feels exhausted and cynical, compassion fatigue or burnout may occur. Both of these exhaustion responses to stress are typically seen in first responders who experience chronic levels of stress in their profession.

Burnout & Compassion Fatigue

Our service can lead us to experience complete Burnout or Compassion Fatigue. Both are detrimental to our service but appear differently. Burnout stages are: enthusiasm, stagnation, frustration, and apathy. Burnout emerges over time and potentially has some psychological effects, such as depressive disorders.

Job burnout has three unique dimensions. The first stage, the police officer may feel like all of the potential resources are exhausted. The individual is at "the end of their rope." The next phase consists of an emotional detachment between the police officer and those who are served by that police officer. The behavior of the police officer may demonstrate as indifference or cynicism. Finally, the last stage is a complete dissatisfaction with any job accomplishments. The police officer may feel like all of the investment into that police officer's work has been a waste of energy and effort and that he or she is completely unsupported by community or organization. In this stage, the officer may choose to turn that dissatisfaction inward, which may lead to depressive behavior. However, the police officer may choose to act outwardly and seek to "get back" at those who are not showing "support." The officer may succumb to unethical or corrupt behavior, expressing if no one cares or values that officer then why should that officer care. Corruption becomes an easy choice and just as easy to justify.

Compassion fatigue is a process, which occurs over time, sometimes taking months or years to appear. The individual suddenly realizes that his or her ability to feel and care has decreased, hope and humor have disappeared, and fatigue is pronounced (Figley, 1999). Many times those who experience compassion fatigue are hardworking and deeply caring individuals. With the chronic levels of stress endured in a service profession, those individuals may experience hopelessness and a decrease in experiencing pleasure. There may be a negative attitude as well. Both compassion fatigue and burnout symptoms appear similar. However, compassion fatigue centers around the actual repeated exposure to the trauma, whereas burnout is focused on the aspects of the job and organization and the individual's perspective of how they are treated.

Again, there has been little direct training with police officers about how to help prevent, treat, or prepare for chronic stress issues. Some of this is due to the secrecy or solidarity of the police culture and some is created by a lack of understanding about the effects of stress on the police officer. Oftentimes police officers consider themselves invincible only to find they are just as vulnerable but completely unprepared. Many times, police officers are simply afraid to admit they are suffering from burnout or compassion fatigue. Frequently, police officers say that they "survived it" so the newer police officers can survive it as well. However, education offers police officers the opportunity to understand both of these severe stress responses, how to prepare for them, and then to seek out solutions should they find themselves in burnout or compassion fatigue.

Post-Traumatic Stress Disorder

Currently, there is a significant amount of stress placed on police officers. There are officers who are working under extreme conditions, such as shortages of personnel, persistent trauma observed daily, and abuses perpetrated from the streets and within the organization. Many of our new police officers already come to the profession with a high level of trauma incurred or observed. In a study of new police recruits, their experiences with trauma were similar to those police officers having ten years or more of service in police work (Violanti, 1999). So our police officers are already impacted by stress and trauma before their first day on the job.

Post-traumatic stress disorder can occur when an individual is exposed to one or more traumatic or significant threat events. With this definition, it begs the question as to why all police officers are not "diagnosed" with this specific anxiety disorder. One answer is the resilience of these individuals. Most police officers understand that the work entails many difficult, if not horrific incidents. Because there is a significant amount of authority and control, many police officers have strong beliefs that they have the capacity to employ influence on the outcomes of those events. For example, a police officer responding to a brutal homicide scene has the belief that he or she will do everything possible to catch that suspect who committed that crime.

This type of perceived control is associated with many positive results as demonstrated in greater mental and physical health (Diehl & Hay, 2010). Police work certainly offers individuals a perceived sense of control. However when unprepared or exhausted, an officer may observe something that becomes very emotionally charged. For example, a police officer responding to a report of missing ten year-old female may not be prepared to deal with the subsequent events of learning the child was actually abducted, then murdered, and then dismembered. That police officer may then begin to experience nightmares, flashbacks, and disturbances in cognitive thoughts. There could be depression associated with the symptoms. The police officer can become dysfunctional, depressed, and even suicidal without intervention.

Here is where we fail not only our police officers but our military as well. We do not "teach" those who will experience this type of trauma about how those experiences may affect them. Without proper training, the extremes create an opportunity for the police officer to "freeze" in that stress or traumatic memory, allowing that memory to sit at the base of the cerebellum in the brain.

So, let me present an over simplification of how a traumatic event may create an opportunity for the individual to develop PTSD (Post-Traumatic Stress Disorder). Perhaps the traumatic event is an officer who experiences a tremendous threat to his safety, such as a deadly force encounter. That officer has a memory of this traumatic event and has attached highly charged emotions around that memory. While we do not know where this memory will reside in the brain, we can assume there are areas of the brain that may activate with this memory.

Our human brain has developed into three distinct areas. The cerebellum is considered the oldest area and sits right at the base of our skull attached to our spinal area. This area controls our physiological functions, such as breathing, heart rate, and coordinated movement. Then the next area, I refer to as our "animal" or mammalian brain. This mid brain area is the next to develop in a human being. In the mammalian brain, we have the limbic system. This system is centered around our ears, deep inside the brain. Here we are hard-wired for anger, fear, and aggression. This brain helps us respond like an animal by the "fight or flight" response. It is our survival center.

The newest portion of our brain is called the neo-cortex or pre-frontal cortex. This area of the brain is right behind our forehead. This brain is our higher executive functioning. We use this area in the brain to problem solve or analyze. Here is where we can find hope and compassion as well as our ethics and morals. It is the last area of the brain to develop in the human being and is usually not completely developed until our mid-twenties. In this area of the brain, we respond by higher thinking and analysis of potential solutions. We can visualize consequences.

So when the police officer experiences a highly emotionally charged event, the memory can get "stuck" in the oldest part of the brain that deals with the basic physiological functions. I often refer to this section of the brain as the "reptilian brain," similar to the alligator that "freezes" on top of the water or down on the bottom of the water when there is a threat. There is almost no motion, a freezing whether predator or prey. The memory is frozen in this area and the police officer does not want to deal with the memory so it sits motionless. Yet, the memory becomes reactivated repeatedly with the strong emotion attached to it. The officer begins to experience the nightmares, flashbacks, and disturbances in thought processes. That tiny portion of the brain actually dies with repeated reactivation.

However, when we debrief the situation, event, or memory we can then move that memory forward from the base of the skull to the frontal lobes into higher level thinking areas of the brain. As the memory is "debriefed" or talked about, the emotion begins to lessen and fade. The memory can then be stored without the emotions attached to it that caused the officer to be emotionally charged. Here is where we can affect change in PTSD.

Yet, we do not explain to our police officers and military how important it is to address the trauma and deal with it as quickly as possible. We shame individuals because they cannot "handle" the trauma. Those police officers/military remain silent because of feeling inadequate that they have been changed by the trauma. Yet, our abilities to become affected and traumatized are what make us human.

The most effective treatment for post-traumatic stress disorder is to address it quickly. If the individual can get therapy after the recognition of the distress in behavior, there is a significant chance that those symptoms can lessen or be eliminated. The ability of our brains to develop neural pathways around the damaged areas is well documented. However, should there be no therapy then the damage remains, the symptoms usually worsen, and the despair may accelerate for the individual. So why would we not choose to educate our police officers and military about what may happen when confronted by trauma?

Psychology of Police

When we look at the types of individuals who choose to work as police officers or first responders, we see some similarities in behavior. Through my research over the last fifteen years, I have recorded that most police officers choose to be in the profession out of a true desire to "help" others. Many of these officers feel "called" to do this type of work. Certainly I felt my police profession was a "calling" for me.

However, the job comes with a variety of stressors, traumas, perspectives, and injurious situations that change us at the cellular level. For example, I was a police officer for 27 years. Currently, that means I have worked as a cop for about half of my life. I am forever changed. I see many situations very differently than my family and friends who have not been in police work. I still look at the exits and entry points in a classroom or restaurant in order to defend against a threat. I often explore "what if" scenarios in my mind, particularly when teaching at the community college, thinking how I can protect and defend the classroom. I feel compelled to go toward the threat rather than run from it. Therefore, the psychology of police is a significant topic to explore as the profession changes one to the soul.

Many young people enter the police profession and want to help. Then they are immediately confronted with inconsistent information. Many times the public that we are sworn to protect appears to hate us, does not want us anywhere around them, and has the potential to kill us. It is interesting to note that in police work there is never a defined "front line" in the fight against crime. Police officers work around their neighbors, storeowners, and other community members. Any one of those members can be the criminal or the enemy. Any one of those individuals may want to harm or kill the police officer. A sense of paranoia can emerge with a lack of an established front line.

Another inconsistency that is important to understand is that in order for police officers to do their job, they have to break some laws. This becomes the new norm for the young police officer. Usually there is an understanding as to when an officer can break the law as taught by training officers, police academies, and the police organization. However, there can be a misinterpretation that the police officer is then "above the law." Sometimes, police officers begin to think about "how much can I get away with?" Most police officers understand that those laws that they may break are to help achieve the goal of stopping criminal activity or prevention of crime. But immaturity or corruption in a police officer can provide an opportunity to push beyond the boundaries or limits in the profession and foster unethical or illegal behavior.

Police officers are taught early on to maintain control of their emotions. They are told to compartmentalize the job, not to share with family or friends outside the job, and to trust no one other than their peers. We effectively turn off these new police officers' abilities to function normally. This type of education is exhausting in order to maintain that type of control for endless hours, months, and years. Then we fail to teach police officers how to re-engage their feelings and emotions, to share with others, and to integrate their work into their lives. We effectively create robots that may blow apart when they cannot maintain that behavior after years of compartmentalized behavior.

This is very similar to our military and to many abusive homes in the world. Powers (2004) stated that our law enforcement officers, military forces, as well as many families share three common rules: "Don't talk, don't trust, don't feel." In persistence of this dysfunctional behavior, we have created a substantial barrier of isolation for the individual. Within that isolation, there is a reduction in objectivity, effective coping behaviors, and positive social support.

Police officers are taught to maintain a high level of vigilance during their shift. However, we fail to tell our police officers about the effects of maintaining that high level of awareness. Certainly, that high alert perspective is imperative in police work. Police officers are the watchdogs of our communities, maintaining awareness and protecting the public. Nevertheless, when an individual operates at such a high level of awareness there are consequences to the health of the individual.

Gilmartin (2002) discusses the effects of hypervigilence and how the body reacts to that vigilence. It is important for police officers to understand that when an individual spends 8-10 hours in that state of hypervigilence, then the body must go below the normal level of vigilence for several hours in order to return to normal vigilence. This low level of vigilence may appear as someone who is "zoned" out in front of the television, not engaged in communicating with family and friends, and appearing disinterested.

Most of our officers return to work sooner than their bodies can recover, lending to enduring states of fatigue and wear and tear on the individual. The same may be true for our military and those individuals in abusive homes. However, we have failed to educate our first responders, military personnel, and others who experience abusive behavior about how heightened states of vigilence can erode health and wellbeing. Therefore, it is important to provide information and education about how individuals are affected by stress and trauma to combat frustration, apathy, and "dis-ease."

Most research in the police culture during the last few decades has focused on the effects of trauma and stress on police officers' lives. It is understood that police work is one of the most stressful professions and the research has concentrated on stress and trauma in the police officer. Yet, relatively little research has focused on how officers survive and thrive in police work. If there are over 655,000 police officers and over 110,000 federal officers, it is important to note that many of those officers survive and even thrive in the profession. The significance of examining how these officers are able to handle the stressors of the job is very important.

The research done by a few of us has focused on why most police officers are able to manage the stress and trauma. In over 150 qualitative interviews with police officers from the United States and the United Kingdom, there were common themes that emerged that may provide the best answers as to how police officers can remain hopeful and resilient (Charles, 2005; Smith & Charles, 2010; Charles, et al., 2014). The first theme was that the police officer believed they were "called" to do the work. Therefore, those traumatic or stressful experiences were viewed as opportunities for positive growth.

The second theme in their narratives was the importance of a humanistic approach to their work. These officers were inclined to "see" the individual in front of them as a human being rather than a criminal or enemy or object. Humanism afforded them the ability to understand that those people who had committed whatever evil acts were still human beings and should be treated fairly and justly.

Finally, those police officers interviewed believed that there was something larger than themselves or beyond themselves. They understood that there was justice on earth and a much larger picture beyond "man's justice." This was consistent regardless of the spiritual belief system, to include atheists (Charles, 2005; Smith & Charles, 2010).

The police officers interviewed in our research were not educated or trained to think or act in the manner described in the preceding paragraphs. This was part of their ability to cope with stress and trauma, transforming those experiences into positive growth rather than succumbing to the effects of stress. While the numbers interviewed to date are not statistically representative of all police officers in the world, we could infer from our results that the same themes emerging in these police officers from two separate continents may represent possible concepts and solutions for helping police officers endure the stress and trauma of the work. It is important to teach our first responders to reflect on how and why police work is important to them. Then we need to educate them as to what changes may occur in their lives due to stress and trauma and how to effectively cope with stress and trauma. The result is we create healthier police officers and begin to heal our police communities.

<u>Stress Questions</u>
1. What are your coping skills and mechanisms?
2. What are some ways that you address your self-care?
Example: Eat healthy foods, exercise regularly
3. How do you feel? Are you experiencing any symptoms of being overly stressed, overly traumatized, or disconnected from family/friends?

CHAPTER 6

Compassion & Re-engagement

"When beyond belief, Believe beyond"
Ginger Charles

Importance of Compassion

September 24, 2015, Pope Francis addressed the United States Congress. In his unprecedented speech, Pope Francis referenced the Golden Rule: to do unto others, as we would have others do onto us. He stated, "If we want opportunity, let us give opportunity. If we want security then let us give security. If we want peace, then let us be givers of peace." Let us have a passion and compassion of service. This is the pursuit of the common good.

When looking for the common good in our police communities, I quickly found myself thinking back to my last assignment before I retired from law enforcement. I was assigned as the sergeant in our Criminal Investigations Bureau, supervising the Crimes Against Persons Detectives and the Crimes Against Children Investigators. I had never served as a detective during my tenure in law enforcement. So, I also needed to learn how to conduct a good criminal investigation, not just a patrol investigation.

I met some of the most remarkable men and women in my last assignment. I was their supervisor, yet they had to do double time to teach me how to conduct an investigation, conduct their investigation, and train me "how they wanted to be supervised." That did not mean they were unsupervised. In fact, they were disciplined police officers/detectives. They had a strong sense of commitment, passion, and compassion for their work. My job was finding the resources they needed to do their work, to offer guidance from a supervisory standpoint, to objectively view their work, and to provide opportunity for growth either in their current position or another.

However, what really stuck with me was these police officers (detectives and investigators) did not have the typical sense of "us versus them" that is so common in police work. There was not a division between whom they worked with and whom they served. During my tenure as a police officer, I never adopted the mentality of "us versus them" approach to police work. I believed that each person I contacted was a relative of mine and should be treated with dignity and respect, even if they were insulting, abusive, a criminal, or evil. So, now I had a wonderful opportunity to work with a group of men and women who viewed police work from the same sense of humanity.

I remember a very seasoned homicide detective telling me that he does not get to pick who his victims are, that he works for his victims regardless of the type of individual they were. Many of these investigators worked their cases to the detriment of health and family. I was a witness to this commitment during the first homicide case I supervised. The detective began his investigation by first needing to teach me what he needed, then coordinating the investigative efforts. After many hours and late into the night, he and I met with the family members of our homicide victim. I remember he told me how important it was to meet with the victim's family. When we met with the family, they were devastated and raw. He soothed them emotionally and emphasized the importance of catching the suspect, who was the son of the victim. He solicited their help in bringing a solid case to the criminal courts.

Throughout the investigation, we met with those family members often, informing them of recent updates to the case and next the steps in the investigation. He "became" a family member, regardless of the victim's behavior before death. He treated the victim and the victim's family with respect and compassion. He was actively involved in their lives for over two years while the case progressed through the courts, ending in conviction of the accused family member.

While he is an excellent investigator, his approach is typical of many of the detectives who truly care about their work and those they serve. I watched another homicide investigator become good friends with one of his victim's family. He spent time at their barbeques and other family functions. He made frequent phone calls to check on family members, even though they lived out of state and the court case had concluded. He invited them to his family events as well. In another example, one investigator would often visit the crime scene after the crime scene tape was removed. He would park his car, sit, and pray for the victim(s). He would ask that they be taken care of and that he do his best work.

These men and women in the criminal investigations bureau demonstrated to me time and again the power of compassion in furthering their meaning and purpose in their work. Each case was not just a job but was a face of someone who needed help. Their work seemed to integrate them into the lives of their victim, yet they remained objective, understanding the importance of their work. They got to know their community. There is a true sense of love for their work. They continued to demonstrate grace, kindness, harmony, and respect for life.

However, they were susceptible to compassion fatigue or burnout. They suffered from colds or flu. They ate poorly and did not exercise enough. Sometimes they did not sleep enough. Herein lies the importance of the supervisor. It is imperative to provide resources for these men and women, to educate them on how to care for themselves, and to give them rest when needed.

Unfortunately, much of the time supervisors may pile on the work or unfairly distribute work because one individual is better at completing cases than another. And, we burn out these officers/detectives. If the supervisor is inexperienced about the work of the investigator and not aware enough of those shortcomings, he or she may add to this compassion fatigue or burnout of the officer or investigator.

From my own experiences, I worked as a Community Resource Officer for several years. One of my duties was to look for ways to engage with our community, to partner with them and problem solve issues in the neighborhoods. I was assigned to an area that had an increase in Russian immigrants. When I would drive through the area, I was confronted with two to three women standing by the curb yelling at me as I drove through the neighborhood. I was very confused by their behavior but I could not understand them, nor could they understand me.

I shared my experiences with my peers and we realized that we had a potential problem for that community as well as ourselves because of the language barrier. I just found my next community issue to tackle. I did some quick research on the situation. I found out that the local church in that area was sponsoring Russian families, helping them immigrate to the United States. The families had a year to establish that they could find work and be self-sufficient. However, there did not appear to be a formalized process where the community could learn English.

I asked my fellow police officers about their experiences with the Russian community. As expected, there were significant frustrations when trying to get information or to communicate with them because of the language difficulties. There were also safety concerns as well when officers and community members cannot understand each other.

I decided to ask my police agency if we could hire an instructor to teach some of us the Russian language. My agency agreed and six other police officers and I took language lessons for about six months. While none of us became proficient, we each were able to say, "hello" and ask a few questions to help us determine how to serve them. I found that when I spoke just one or two words of Russian in this community, the tension seemed to decrease significantly.

Later, we presented our language program to the Problem Oriented Policing Conference in San Diego, California. However, the lesson for me was how we cared enough about a community that we attempted to find a way to communicate. We did not get any extra pay or honors. We just wanted to help. The program kept police officers and the community safe and allowed us to understand each other, even minimally. Tibetan Buddhist nun, Pema Chodron said it perfectly, "Compassion is not a relationship between the healer and the wounded. It's a relationship between equals. Only when we know our own darkness well can we be present with the darkness of others. Compassion becomes real when we recognize our shared humanity."

Forgiveness

When we hold onto hurts and slights, we become burdened by the weight of these wounds. Police officers are subjected to abuse and trauma each day of service. Many times, these police officers experienced high levels of abuse in their own homes before becoming a police officer. Many of the police officers I have interviewed have described growing up in unsafe homes. Oftentimes, that was the motivation leading them to serve as a police officer. One participant from our research revealed his upbringing of abuse as he illustrated the importance of his commitment to serve and protect:

> *I just dedicated my life to [the victims]; I get teary eyed when I think of this. I just thought these folks [the victims] reminded me of my sister and I hunkered down in the corner of a bedroom waiting for my stepfather to cut my sister's eyes out. I just identified with them and some of them were pains in the ass, to say the least* (Charles, 2005; Charles, 2009).

There is a healing power of forgiveness when we choose to take our experiences and move ourselves toward helping others. Some of that power is self empowerment, taking control of the situation and working towards integrating those experiences to personal transformation.

Teel describes the strength of forgiveness by bringing "any wounds from your past into the light of day" (2014, p 202), that there is significance in writing about your experiences. With the inherent secrecy in police work, we often have undisclosed trauma and hurts that reflect our three rules of don't talk, don't trust, and don't feel. Yet, when we carry our secrets, the weight becomes unbearable after years of burying and holding those secrets. And, this is true of our marginalized communities as well.

There is such empowerment to write about our experiences as police officers. Oftentimes, the opportunity to offer words of wisdom to others, to mentor and teach each other through a learned subject is life changing. Those who are changed by our words also change us and create opportunity and growth. This growth allows us to change at the cellular level, helping to develop neural pathways in the brain that lead to hope, compassion, empathy, and health rather than pockets of despair, apathy, depression, and cynicism.

From a sense of service, it is very important to nurture oneself and take care of the soul. Nurturing our inner soul or spirit may sound like "fluff" for hardened police officers. However, when we don't take care of self there is no taking care of anyone else. Some may see this as a selfish pursuit. However, there is some research in behavioral health risks that has shown some correlation with women who are singularly focused on a goal (such as family) and high in self deception (stating that there is nothing wrong, everything is fine when it's not) and being diagnosed with breast cancer (Wickramasekera, 1988). The reasons may be as simple as a denial of what is going on inside, denying our own needs, and powering through life rather than self reflecting on our own health concerns.

Forgiveness Questions
1. Can you forgive? Yourself?
2. What would it take to forgive?
3. What might change if you could forgive?

Challenge & Change of Police

As of December 2015, police have shot and killed 965 civilians (Rich & Kelly, 2015). In 2014, police killed 1100 people while violent crime was at an all time low. In 2013, 763 people were killed by the police in the United States. By comparison, the United Kingdom killed one person in 2014, have not had a fatal shooting this year, and from 2010 through 2014 had four fatal shootings in a population of 52 million people. Other countries reflect similar numbers. In Germany, police killed no one between 2014 through 2015. Iceland police have killed only one person … ever.

Americans have a significant gun culture. We are particular violent and punitive in the United States and we are armed to the teeth. I understand there are reasons why we have this gun culture and that it is not going away. However, that does not mean that we should not examine if there are better ways of managing our obsession with firearms. The consequences of not exploring alternatives or potential solutions would be no changes, a continuation of the same results, the same arguments played over and again.

While interviewing police officers in the United States and the United Kingdom, there was usually a discussion concerning police officers being armed or unarmed. From my own experiences and interviews with other U.S. police officers, it is unimaginable to think about policing this country without a firearm. It is a brave symbol of our authority and strength as a police force. Yet, police officers in the United Kingdom shared with me that they consider their service brave for not carrying a firearm. In fact, each year there is an opportunity to vote as to whether they should begin to carry firearms. Each year it has been voted down by their national police force.

So here is our challenge. Here is our need to change. There are approximately 18,000 police agencies in the country. All of these agencies have armed police officers. We, as a country, are armed or have the "right to" arm ourselves. And, there is tremendous distrust of our police force. It is time to explore solutions.

For example, in the 2014 shooting of Laquan McDonald, police officer Jason Van Dyke fired his weapon sixteen times, killing McDonald. There were several other officers on scene, yet no other officers fired their weapon. McDonald was armed with a knife but was not approaching the officers as observed on police video. The question arises as to other options available to the officers. Why were there no tasers used in this scenario? Are all police officers issued tasers or do the officers need to call for a taser. Chicago Police Department is not the only police organization where police officers must call for a taser or some other less lethal use of force.

If each police officer is not issued a taser and must call for one, there are interesting ramifications with this decision. First, we must be cognizant about whether the police officer will have time to call for a taser, wait for that taser to arrive on scene, and then deploy the tool. Second, why would a police agency arm its police officers with firearms or require that officer be armed with a handgun yet not issue each officer a taser, which is a less lethal use of force? Are we not, in fact, handicapping our police officers by not providing alternative solutions to deadly force?

Our police officers and police organizations are currently facing a level of violence and tension from our communities that we have not seen before. For many years, police officers enjoyed a level of public trust that is no longer as prominent, particularly in our marginalized communities. To be a police officer in this day is a tremendous challenge. Our police officers need to be well trained and provided with additional tools that offer solutions to de-escalate, to think and problem-solve rather than to just react.

Police officers now must help ease these challenges and conflicts. The concept of service certainly resonates now. Our young men and women who are choosing the profession of policing have the opportunity to truly help those in our struggling communities. The future police officer must have the understanding that the community must be engaged with the work of the police officer and the police officer must connect with community as well. Otherwise, the violence and tension will continue.

Systemic vs. Individual Changes

Zimbardo (2008) discussed that one of the reasons we saw the atrocities in Abu Ghraib was due to social psychological effects of the situation rather than the dispositional nature of the soldiers. He lectured about the importance of viewing evil from a "public health" approach rather than a "medical model" approach. The concept is very applicable here in the police communities. We must look at the issues in our police organizations from a systemic approach.

For example, I witnessed at my own agency where an investigation revealed several crimes and integrity issues involving several front line police officers. Some of the command staff stated, "I did not do this" or "this isn't my fault." When the command staff began looking at how this behavior was allowed to exist, these commanders and police executives quickly distanced themselves from the police officers and their behavior. Unfortunately, it was imperative that these police leaders accept responsibility for the behavior of their troops rather than distancing themselves.

I tried to address some of these behavioral issues with some of these same police officers years before these integrity issues resurfaced. However, the commander I worked for at the time chose to minimize the behavior. I knew this unethical behavior would continue, that we just moved the behavior under the surface, and it would reappear with intensity. While I left that supervisory position and went on to another supervisory assignment in the agency, those same officers continued their behavior. When the criminal and unethical behavior reappeared five years later, it was worse and significantly affected several police officers' careers, damaged the trust of the citizens who were directly affected, and left many in our agency wondering how this could happen in our organization.

Unfortunately, it happens in many of our police organizations and is not unusual in the police culture. We just refuse to admit that it could happen until it surprises us and the bad behavior rears its ugly head. Here is where we can change this outcome. We must recognize this is a systemic problem and not a "bad apple" or one bad individual. We have to change the system because that will change the individual. If the culture or community does not accept the criminal or unethical behavior and then discipline accordingly, then the opportunities lessen for the behavior to flourish. That requires our police leaders to look at their own behavior, the culture's behavior, and the organization's values.

The command officers who said they were not a part of the problem actually then become the problem. There were a few other supervisors who happened to be supervising the "bad apples" at the time the criminal and unethical behavior was uncovered. They were disciplined for their part. Yet, there were other supervisors who had supervised those same officers. Again, behavior was overlooked or unaddressed. I remember telling one of the sergeants who was disciplined that the problem was not just their fault, that we all must share in the fault and behavior of the organization. It is critical to look at the entire organization's behavior and culture in order to change it systemically. We can hire and fire police officers when they "go bad" but that never addresses the absolute problem or the root of the issue because an opportunity or a situation will emerge again.

Certainly, when reviewing the events at Abu Ghraib, there was a distancing of our military leaders, allowing for the soldiers to begin to extend and push the boundaries of their authority. These soldiers were inexperienced and ill prepared for the position they were serving. They were frustrated and alone. They were working at night without any authority overseeing their behavior. Their behavior became sadistic and twisted.

The Stanford Prison Experiment (Zimbardo, 2007) demonstrated this concept by taking young men, psychologically, mentally, and physically healthy and turning the those young males who were guards into sadistical abusers. The young men who were prisoners suffered mental, physical, emotional distress and within seven days, the experiment was stopped. Several of the "prisoners" experienced breakdowns. This experiment has now become a tremendous demonstration of what can happen when we place people in positions of authority, without oversight, training, and experience, expecting them to do good work. This demands that our police leaders be involved and engaged in what is happening in the organization and with each police officer.

CHAPTER 7

How Do You Want to Be Policed?

"The police are the public and the public are the police; the police being only members of the public who are paid to give full time attention to duties, which are incumbent on every citizen in the interests of community welfare and existence."
Sir Robert Peel

I so clearly remember my lesson from that police chief constable from his interview in May 2010. The United Kingdom National Police Services began asking their communities how they wanted to be policed years ago. I have often thought about this perspective. In fact, my fascination with behavior probably had me thinking about how we police people before I was properly "schooled" by this police leader.

When I worked as a police officer in a small mountain town, my police agency decided to conduct surveillance on the homeless camps to determine who was buying alcohol for the underage kids in our community. We had several incidents where teenagers were involved in alcohol overdose or driving under the influence. Through a preliminary investigation, we discovered that it appeared our homeless population was purchasing alcohol for our young people and then receiving alcohol for payment.

During the surveillance, we recorded some of the conversation in the homeless camps. Many of the homeless identified (by name) those police officers that treated them fairly, regardless of whether they were served a ticket or taken to jail by these police officers. They described the importance of being treated like a human being and how that formed their opinion of the police officer. The examples shared by these men were of officers who actually "saw" them, viewed them as human beings rather than trash, and spoke with them. These homeless men shared with each other that they would "help" these officers if they were ever in trouble. I was fortunate to be one of the officers these homeless men believed treated them fairly. This made a tremendous impression on my soul as there were many times I worked the entire city alone as the only police officer on duty for hours late into the night. In fact, there were times I was the only officer working in the entire county. So, I recognized early on the importance of enforcement with compassion, of education rather than punishment, of respect and humanism. It was not just morally correct but helped me survive.

In 2010 that police leader reminded me of the importance of asking how our communities should be policed, engaging community in solutions. Those police officers named years ago by the homeless men as "mean" or "bad" were identified as brutal in how they were treated by them, that they were less than human, less than animals. They described these officers purposefully destroying their cardboard homes. They were clear in the conversations with each other that should those officers ever need help, they would walk away without assisting. These men never said they would do harm to the officers but were clear that they would never help them.

So how do we, as individuals or communities, want to be policed? I thought it important to ask some individuals who were willing to participate in a conversation about policing issues. These people can be described as coming from marginalized communities or very familiar with marginalized communities. They have chosen to be brave and stand up and say, "This is how I want to be policed!" They describe having been directly affected by the police culture and offer their viewpoint in this section. These individuals are part of the solution for our police communities. I asked them questions about their experiences with police, how they wanted to be policed, and what solutions they saw helping heal the divide between the police and marginalized communities. Then I let them talk.

Barry Graves

I met Barry at an event at Modesto Junior College in Modesto, California. Barry had decided to perform a "spoken word piece" in front of the audience just before the event. It was not part of the schedule. This spoken word piece could be described as a poetry sharing. His words were powerful and challenging about his beliefs around what is happening between the police and community. He compared approaches from Martin Luther King and Malcolm X and "turning the other cheek" or "by any means possible." Behind him stood two local police leaders. I felt the tension in the crowd, the apprehension of some, and the fear of others. I chose to interview Barry and he agreed.

I asked him if he believed he was from a marginalized community. He quickly answered "yes," but asked what I meant by marginalized. I told him I was interested in his definition and belief about marginalized communities. He said he grew up just on the edge of the projects and he equated a safe neighborhood as the lack of police presence; that if police officers were around that meant the neighborhood it was not safe. Barry described when he was in Hunter's Point, a project neighborhood in Northern California, he understood that the presence of police meant that something bad could happen.

Barry said he identified police using "motorbikes" in the projects as a way of catching criminals. The projects were up on a hillside and the 'motorbikes" were able to climb the hills more effectively than an officer in a patrol car. Barry shared that some community members considered his family rich but he said his entire family worked very hard and they lived in an apartment or townhouse or house just on the edge of what some considered bad areas. He continued by saying, "you only know you're in a bad neighborhood when you see a lot of police."

He has several family members from the law enforcement community. His great grandfather was one of the first black municipal court judges appointed in San Francisco and his grandfather was a police detective with the San Francisco Police Department in the Fraud Division. Barry's family has an extensive background in law enforcement and military, yet his performance at the event the night I met him described a deep wounding from that same community.

As Barry was answering my questions, I asked a clarifying question for myself. I asked Barry how he wanted to be identified. I said I have asked this question before as to whether someone wanted to be identified as an African American or Black American or black. Barry shared that he has thought a great deal about that very question. He said he knows he has brown skin. He has been called, "Black, Nigger, 'Nigga,' a nappy head, just a number of names." He stated he knows his name is Barry, his father's name is Barry, and his son's name is Barry. He said he just does not know how to identify himself. Then he said, "I know that I have brown skin, I know I have black hair, but I'm so much more than my skin color."

His response hit me right in the face. He is so right. I asked this question as a researcher identifying a participant, using a proper term. His response was a tremendous reminder that we are so much more than just our appearance.

I remember one of the participants from my research with police officers shared a similar experience. He said he was transporting an intoxicated male to the jail after arresting him for some minor charge. He said he asked the male, "How long have you been a drunk?" The male responded, "How long have you been a pig?" This officer realized his poor attempt at talking with this man was simply insulting. He said the moment defined him. While my question was directed in identifying Barry with respect as to his heritage, I felt as if I was insulting. He is so much more than his skin color. He is an intelligent, kind, professional, and caring young man.

I then asked Barry if he had any negative encounters with police. Barry said he had, that the first incident happened at a party at a university in Indiana, 2002. He was sprayed with mace by a police officer. He described that he and some other students were late to a sorority party at a performance center on campus. Because they arrived late, they could not enter and had gathered in the parking lot just outside of the center. Other students also arrived late. These students joined Barry and the other students as they talked, gathered phone numbers, and set up other parties. Barry said the police officers suddenly arrived and drove their cars into the area, jumping the curbs and scattering the students. The officers demanded that the students leave immediately.

A band of police officers began walking shoulder-to-shoulder and approached Barry and the other students. He heard one police officer say "get in the car, boy" repeatedly. That was the second time he heard and was called that disparaging word "boy" from a white man in that town. He said something broke inside and he responded, "Who you callin' boy, Bitch. I'm a man!" Barry said the police officer said again, "Get in your car, boy!" He said he must have "flipped him" the middle finger. His friend quickly grabbed him and pulled him to the car telling him, "Barry get in the car, these cops are racist." His friend tried to close the car door but the police officer reached inside the car. The officer said, "It's too late, he's going to jail." The officer grabbed Barry and as he pulled away the police officer sprayed him with mace. He was taken out of the car, handcuffed, and placed on the ground. Another police officer said, "now sit there, boy."

Barry tried to ask them to let him go. He apologized and asked to be let go. His friend told the police to let Barry go, that he did not do anything, and not to hurt him. His friend was then arrested. Barry said a different officer bent down and said in his ear, "I bet you'll think twice before messin' with these white cops, won't you boy." Barry said he could not see because of the chemical spray but he knew it was a black police officer. Barry said he lost it and said he got angry and yelled. Then another police officer came over and told him that it was going to get a lot worse. Barry then again tried to apologize and asked to be let go.

Barry was having trouble breathing and asked to go to the hospital. The police officer told him he was still going to jail once he was treated by a doctor. At the hospital, the doctor asked Barry what was wrong and the police officer told the doctor he was sprayed with mace. Barry said the doctor was not interested in helping him so Barry said to just take him to jail. Once there, they put him with the intoxicated inmates and made him sit there for two to three hours and then just let him go. He was not charged with anything. He was not intoxicated. Barry described this incident with the police occurred on fraternity row where there were many parties. He had observed the parties where this police activity did not happen with "white" community, yet when there was a party with black students the police aggressively reacted.

Barry described a similar incident in the same area. He was with some soccer players just hanging out on the porch when police officers approached and yelled for everyone to get inside and get out of the area. Barry said his back was to the street and he did not realize the police were approaching. He said he yelled some profanities and saw the stunned faces on the other party-goers. Barry turned around to face a very angry white police officer. He described the police officer as "beet red face, sweating, gritting his teeth and nose-to-nose" with Barry. He said the cop said, "What did you say, boy?" Barry told him he was just singing a rock song. The other police officer grabbed his partner and told him to leave it alone. Barry said he turned his back and walked away.

I then asked Barry how he wanted to be policed. He has such an array of experiences from family members in law enforcement to having been arrested, his viewpoint is important. Barry said he wanted to be "policed from a distance." Initially, this answer seemed troubling and not a helpful solution but he explained his answer. He said:

> It would be nice if you were there when I called you. It
> would be nice if I saw you on your feet more than I did
> from a police car. It would be nice if I knew who you

were, if I could put a face and a family to the badge, rather than the family being the badge. If I knew what church you went to and what religion you are. It would be nice if I could count on you knowing the truth rather than enforcing justice of your kind. If you could treat every situation as a special situation, that I matter, my family matters, my community matters because when you kill someone in my community, in my family you lose trust, you violated us: much like the rapist to the raped, much like the oppressed to the oppressor. You're on the other side now. You've crossed the line. It can't be undone. It's not that simple. It can be that simple if I look past your badge, if I look at you like a human being, which you are. I know that you're there and that gives me security, when I call I know you're there. I don't get security from seeing you in an intimidating way. I get fear and that fear places a stress on you. I don't want to feel like if you're mad I may get hurt or if you're angry I may die and not see my kids. That's what I see when I see police.

I asked Barry about solutions for the police community. Barry said we should explore why someone wants to be a police officer.

Is it to serve, is it to protect, is it to help people? I think the way that we solve it is by looking at what made us want to become part of the law because that carries a weight, that carries a responsibility, a heavy responsibility to be judge and jury at a moment's notice and if that's based on race or class or emotion then it stands a high chance of someone being abused or hurt or offended. There is a strong chance of trust being violated. So taking a look at why someone wants to be a police officer and a way to "de-program" any kind of ideologies that were enforced

on you as a child. For example, all black people are bad;
all brown people are not to be trusted. Certain things
that make you stereotype an individual or class, these
things need to be researched before we give someone a
badge. Too many times we look at the psychological tests
or physical tests and see a kid who gets good grades, was
on football team and scored high on the written exam.
We think, let's make him a cop. No reason not to as he's
passed all the requirements on paper. But we just let
someone who thinks all black people should be extermi-
nated, police black people and wear a badge that rep-
resents honor and trust. That's what they represent but
deep down they believe they can advance their personal
belief through their job. They're given certain freedom to
do so. You're giving the key to humanity.

Barry just clearly illustrated a key point. He described the importance of identifying *implicit bias*, those beliefs that lie under the
surface of our conscious thought process. He articulated so well why
this is now important.

He said he believes that communities can police themselves with
the aid of the police. He said that maybe police officers can train community members to be more vigilant and better at recognizing how
to take care of their community and the police would be there when
needed. He believes the police need to share with the community
that they know they have damaged the community's trust but that
the goal is to rebuild and to "partner" with them, perhaps teach them.
Barry said:

For example, here is how to recognize a robbery in prog-
ress or here is how to help diffuse a hostile situation. In
turn, perhaps the community can teach how you talk to
someone in the community or how you approach some-
one who is schizophrenic and needing help.

He said he believes this is a start, to learn from each other. Barry ended the interview by telling me that this is the first time he has been asked these question and his responses taken seriously. He said there was a similar time when a college president asked his opinion about how to improve campus security interactions with students after a violent incident occurred on the campus. According to Barry, those suggestions did not go any further than the discussion.

Barry said he was coached at a young age on how to deal with the police from his cousin who was a drug dealer. He said his cousin told him to talk as "white" as possible and friendly, to say, "Yes sir." He said his cousin said to be happy and smile, to look the officer in the eyes, to sit up straight in the car. He said "that way they don't want to beat you or search you or arrest you."

Barry's interview was so powerful for me. He is such an intelligent, caring, and gentle man. He believes that what is needed is for police officers to let go of the chip on their shoulders. He said that only disconnects police officers from humanity. As he described what is needed, he was very clear that there are such good men and women out there currently serving their communities. Barry knows there are many police officers that do the job as he has suggested in this interview. What he knows is there are those who do not and that has caused the systemic problem in our police communities. His powerful words made me think:

> *Have we considered a mentor, one who takes that*
> *cop into the neighborhood – To learn …*
> *How to Police!*

Professor Albert Smith

Professor Smith teaches history at Modesto Junior College. He agreed to be interviewed and provided great insight and "history" into issues between police community and those they serve. He spent the early part of his "life in all black communities," describing that while segregation was not legal; it was enforced or still practiced. He said, "I came up in a segregated system that made me feel like the 'other' from the very beginning of my consciousness." When he traveled outside of his community, he said he really felt like the "other."

Professor Smith described that he was a child who always asked "why," which soon lead to him receiving mixed signals in his world. He began to understand that he was living in two separate worlds with two different vocabularies, two complete behavioral profiles. He said, "In those days (1960's) there were only so many things you could say to white people without being checked." He laughed as he shared that his grandfather spent a great amount of time with him, teaching him how to talk to white people. He emphasized his love for his grandfather and his mentorship as he was "always stepping out of line."

I commented to him that Barry also described similar mentoring from his cousin about how to talk to "white people." Professor Smith agreed and said that "when the country moved from segregation 'legally' to integration 'legally,' it was very necessary for his community to be "mentored into the mixed society," that it was a very confusing time for the country.

I asked him what his experience had been with the police community. He said:

> Wow, let's start back in Oakland in the early days if you will. I lived in an all black part of Oakland at the time. It was in the sixties and the community had gotten so paranoid from the influx of blacks during the depression and World War II that they began hiring white police officers from the south. So they would come into our communities not even knowing California law. And they'd just be hitting on us ... thumpers. So some of my first experiences ... one time I was when I was coming home from elementary school, I noticed an area blocked off. Then I noticed why it was blocked off. There was a small riot going on and it was all white cops with nightsticks

thumping all blacks citizens. I was probably nine. Those were my experiences.

He continued describing his life growing up during the 1960's in the Bay Area of California. His words were a history lesson for me as well:

Then coming up around that time in Oakland was the Black Panther Party for Self Defense. People forget about that last part of "self defense." The whole idea was that if the community couldn't trust the police then the community would police itself. You had some elements that were criminal but you had some elements that were just angry college students. When they came into my neighborhood, I noticed a change in the vibe in the community because they worked to earn people's trust in the community. They did things that you never hear about in the history books. They'd take grocery money from old ladies and the grocery lists and they'd come back with the groceries and the change! They chased out all the other drug dealers except for them. And, there were no more burglaries in my neighborhood. Just like that they flipped the entire script of policing. Of course they ran afoul with the local law enforcement and the FBI and so the picture that is given of them is once again different than the one I saw when I was growing up. In fact, the first time I ever heard about black history outside of slavery was from them because they operated youth centers. My mother worked in San Francisco. We got out of school at 2:40 and my mom didn't want us wandering the streets so she sent us to the local Catholic church, which had a little after school thing for awhile until about 5:00. Then after that we went to the local youth center, which was run by the local Black Panthers and we had peanut butter

and jelly, chocolate milk, regular milk, and a lesson in
black history. It was pretty cool. I had a wonderful set of
opportunities and at the time this was my neighborhood.
This was my life.

I asked Professor Smith to elaborate a bit further on the concept of
the Black Panther Party and their ability to come into a neighborhood
and "change the vibe." I wondered how long that transition took the
neighborhood to feel the difference. He said it took just months, that the
Black Panthers would roll around the neighborhood in a car with three
or four inside and they were "armed" as it was legal at the time. He said:

When they saw a policeman hassle a member of the
community, they would usually stop and stand or sit in
their car and watch and if they saw anything that was
not 'kosher,' if you will, then they'd confront the officer
and they'd do that with a law book.

So the confrontation involved challenging the police officer's
knowledge about his ability to do the job properly. Professor Smith
said that of course it angered the police officer. It also gave them a
reputation within months and created the change in the community.

Professor Smith shared another experience saying that growing
up in a black neighborhood and predominantly poor neighborhood
gave him the opportunity for many interactions with the police unfortunately. He explained when he was a high school student living
near Fresno in a town called Clovis, he was walking with friends when
they were "lit up" (activating lights and siren) by the police. He said
they were walking because they did not have a car. When the police
stopped them, they were asked where they were coming from and
where they were going. Then it escalated to the police telling them to
take everything out of their pockets and put it on the hood of the police car. He said they had nothing on them nor had they done anything
wrong. The officers then ran clearances on their names to see if they

had any warrants. Professor Smith said they waited for 45 minutes and then the police officers told them they were out after curfew and the police officers were going to "take them in."

He explained that he and his friends were handcuffed and "given the ride." I asked him what he meant by "the ride." He explained the handcuffs were not double-locked. When handcuffs are double-locked, the cuffs do not continue to get tighter on the wrists. He said they were placed in a transport wagon and driven around town for quite awhile and then "pulled up in front of the police department." The police officers opened the doors and said, "Okay you're free." He said his parents were there by that time. We both agreed that his description of this experience appeared to be an illegal detention or harassment. Professor Smith did share that not all his experiences with police have been negative. However, he recognizes there is a police culture that appears more punitive than it needs to be.

I then asked him how he wanted to be policed. He was really amazed by the question, saying that something similar has come up in one of his classes. He said that he wants to be policed from a sense of "public service." He said he clearly knows what that means as he considers himself to be a public servant. He elaborated on his response by saying that "it's not really that hard to humanize the job." His uncle had over 30 years in law enforcement and his father was in the military for 36 years. He said he understands those cultures.

Professor Smith also said he believed that small outposts in the community are a great benefit to the community and policing. He said with just a few officers, they can respond quickly to calls for service and have the ability to really know the people in their communities. He agreed that it is important for the police officer to become fully integrated in the community, that the integration simplifies the process of public service. He said, "I want to know Officer Bob as Officer Bob and I want him to call me Al."

I then asked him for solutions. He had actually asked his students in his classes about viable solutions to this problem in our police community. One student submitted an article with references about the "incidents of female police officers escalating to violence are very slim and if they are paired with a male officer, that it cuts the testosterone down." He thinks that balancing out the teams with female and male officers would help.

Another suggestion he had was also from one of his students. His student had done some research, illustrating that full social maturity does not happen until approximately 25 years of age. Because of this, he suggested there be an age limit and a higher education requirement as prerequisites for entering in the police profession. Professor Smith said this would help with the new officer having more life experience than the individual who enters the profession at 21 years of age.

We concluded the interview with the clear understanding of how important it is to continue working on resolutions within the police community and those communities served. Many of his students have had some negative experiences with our police. He said his work bringing law enforcement and students together at future events continues.

M.E.Ch.A.

I changed the format and interviewed the entire group, asking the same questions of all the attending members. M.E.Ch.A. is a national club in the United States. The acronym stands for Movimiento Estudiantil Chicano de Aztlan. M.E.Ch.A. is considered a "leadership development" group focused on the value of community. I met with them December 2015 to learn about their insights, concerns, and beliefs regarding police and the community. Approximately 10 to 12 club members agreed to speak with me about their stories.

Some members agreed to be identified but did not complete the contact information and release so I was not able to include their names and refer to them as "individual," "student," or "participant." However, all members were engaged in the conversation and added to the content. Their opinions and stories were just as powerful and further illuminated themes that emerged from the other interviews.

I asked the question about whether they would consider themselves as coming from a marginalized community. Approximately 99 percent believe that they have come from a marginalized community. One young female stated that she was raised on an island and felt there were opportunities denied to her, which presented barriers for her. She said she feels the loss of culture with trying to assimilate into the United States. She felt some people were not allowed to assimilate into the United States culture and so they were marginalized. Another individual described a feeling of invisibility, not seeing "people of color," creating feelings of marginalization. A young female student discussed that she came from a culture of gang violence and drugs. In the neighborhoods where she grew up, this behavior was "normal." She recognized that "when the rich people were passing by" she saw the windows in their vehicles go up. She felt the police were in the neighborhood to harass the community. She said instead of feeling safe with the increase of police in the neighborhoods, she "felt scared." Her thoughts centered on whether the police would take her away. The theme of "feeling scared" when there is an increase in police presence has appeared in other narratives.

One student shared that she grew up in the Bay Area of California, in a predominately "white area." She said she could feel the other community members' discomfort with her and her family that "they thought we were going to do something to them or take something from them." Even though her parents were "middle class people," they were viewed with suspicious and fear. She said, "we live in the same neighborhood with you, we live in a good house, it's not like we are going to do anything to you."

I asked the group about their experiences with police, both good and bad. A student shared that where she lives, she noticed a police car drive by and then come back around. This time the police car had her son in the car. She said her son had just left to walk to his friend's house around the corner. It was 9:30 at night and the police officer asked her if the young man was her son. She told him that was her son and asked what he had done. The officer told her that they had found him walking the neighborhood. She told the officer that her son was walking to his friend's house and asked why they brought him home. She felt the contact with her son, who was in high school at the time, was harassment. There was no ticket or citation issued. He was just picked up and taken home, literally blocks from his house.

One participant shared an experience where the police officer stopped her mom driving their car with "expired license tags." She and her siblings were in the car. Her mother did not have her driver's license with her. She explained that she does not believe that all police are "bad." She said this police officer told her mother that she would receive a ticket for the "expired license tags but he was not going to tow the car." The officer explained that he did not want to have her family walking home late at night in an area that was known for high levels of criminal activity. She said she understood the police officer could have taken the car and left them stranded to walk home but he chose to look the other way and let them go.

One young female student said she and her boyfriend were stopped because one of the lights was out in her vehicle. She said the police contact was very personal, questioning her about why she was with her boyfriend. She said her boyfriend was handcuffed while they interviewed both of them. They continued to question her about why she was with her boyfriend. She said he was targeted because of his clothing and the officers kept telling her that she should not be with someone like him. She challenged the police and said she knew the officers were not supposed to be asking questions like that. She and her boyfriend were finally released with a ticket but she felt the contact was beyond the scope of the traffic contact; that it was harassment.

Another individual described that she was stopped for being on her cell phone. She said when the officer stopped her she had already stopped in her driveway. She got out of her car and the police officer demanded that she get back in her car and get her driver's license and vehicle registration. He told her that he had observed her talking on her cell phone while driving. However, her phone was in her purse in the back seat of the vehicle. She told him she was fixing her hairpin and was not on the phone. He said he saw her on her phone but she challenged him to check her purse in the back seat of the car. The officer never checked her purse for her phone.

She said he left to check her driver's license and then returned. When he returned, he asked her if she was going to continue to argue with him. She told him that she was telling him the truth and he could check her phone to see whether she was using it at the time of contact. The police officer then told her that he could handcuff her and take her because she was arguing with him. She said "go for it, I'm not doing anything wrong." The officer returned to his patrol car and wrote her a ticket. When he gave her the ticket he told her that if she had just told him she was on her phone he would not have written her a ticket. She said to him, "Why would I lie to you?" She went to court and showed the judge her call log from the phone company that showed she was not on her phone at the time of the traffic stop but the judge was not interested. She said the paperwork and time to go to court was very expensive so she just gave up and paid the ticket.

I then asked the main question about how this group wanted to be policed. The first individual said he wanted to be policed with "fairness," "truth," and "equity." He said he has been a police officer and understands the culture. He said he also knows what it is like to be "profiled." His approach was to challenge the officer on the reason for the contact. However, he was speaking from his experiences as a police officer. He said, "It is so important to be policed with fairness, truth, and equity."

One student said she felt that policing from a distance is important. The concept of policing from a distance was suggested by other participants' interviews. Her concern was the police jumping to conclusions and not exploring all the circumstances. Three students discussed militarization of police and excessive force and how that interferes with how they would like to be policed. While they agreed that with an active shooter situation or mass-shooting disaster, the use of militarized tactics is very appropriate. However, to use this type of equipment or tactics on community members is not appropriate from their perspective.

When I asked for solutions to help resolve the conflict between the police community and those they serve, one young female said "more training in policing people of color." This is a dynamic concept when other participants have stated that they were "mentored" in how to talk with "white people." These students believe perhaps a full training course in recognition of biases, how to talk with "people of color," and building community relations would help. The recognition of the human element is very important to them ..., as it should be.

Another student shared how her perspective has changed since her brother-in-law was recently hired as a police officer. She said:

> *Cops used to be viewed with respect. They provided safety and they maintained order. They were 'the law' and were actually trusted to follow the law ... but perhaps somewhere along the way they lost respect for us as human beings so we lost respect for them. "Freedom" became only a word without a definition; meaning if at any point in time we had freedom of speech, freedom of religion, freedom of self, we lost it and we are no longer free. Now we, or I, as a Chicana woman of color living in the States live with worry that on any given day I can be stopped, searched, or taken for no reason.*

One young male talked about his contact with police when he was running for exercise at night. The officer contacted him and told him that he saw the young man looking inside vehicles. The young man told the officer that he was "running for exercise." The officer called him a "Spic" and grabbed him. The young man pulled away from the officer. He said fortunately a woman witnessed the contact from her porch and told the officer to leave him alone. When the officer recognized this woman witnessed the contact, he told this young man to "watch his back" and got in his car and left. This young man said he was told that the officer was fired for his behavior as he had acted the same way with other individuals.

When these students discussed that they want to be "policed from a distance," I recognized most of these participants have had situations where they have not felt "free" to move in their own communities. Because some police officers had harassed them or "swarmed" into their neighborhoods, they were left feeling fearful rather than safe. This is significant for us to understand how police behavior may create such an atmosphere of fear.

In a final comment from the group, one young man pointed out that instead of color it "becomes 'blue' and then everyone else." He believed that makes it more difficult to police people, regardless of color. His comment is significant in pointing out the "us versus them" mentality that may befall the police culture.

I ended my interview with this group of young men and women. What was very apparent was while most of the experiences with the police community were negative, their hope was not lost. They wanted to know where the "good" police officers are. They believe, as stated in the other two interviews, that policing from a distance is one solution.

Common emerging themes

The first theme I heard in each of these interviews was the concept of "policing from a distance." When I first heard these words, I was somewhat alarmed. The concept does not "fit" into the public safety schema. However, as they expanded their theory, I began to understand. They were asking for trust from the police community. They wanted the opportunity to work as partners with the police and monitor their own community members' behavior, calling when they needed help.

If we evaluate healthy parenting, we can see this type of behavior and suggested solution is normal. I immediately had an image of "helicopter parents" overwhelming their children; those parents who refuse to allow their children to grow beyond their reach. Healthy parenting allows the child to explore boundaries, gently guiding the child back in line when that child violates a boundary. While our community members are not children, the opportunity to educate, discipline, and mentor those members is imperative and important. When the police officer is an authoritarian personality, there is no space for providing an understanding between police and community. There is only room for punishment for failure to follow the rules.

The participants were all clear that they knew the police were there to help them but did not need police presence overwhelming them, intimidating them, and controlling their movements. Baltimore (Wallace-Wells, 2015) had an opportunity to experience this concept after the violence and activism surrounding Freddy Gray's death. In some parts of the city, the police seemed to retreat and were less visible. Homicides dramatically increased in the area. A lieutenant colonel in Baltimore Police Department, Melvin Russell, then met with an unusual group that included representatives from some of the major gangs in Baltimore. The meeting involved working toward solutions to ease the violence in the city.

Baltimore Lieutenant Colonel Russell asked the gang members to help him disperse the crowds each night (Wallace-Wells, 2015). Each night those representatives from most of the gangs met him at a specific corner in the city to help the police and the community through the unrest and violence. The participants who were interviewed in this book also discussed the importance of police helping community members "police" themselves, offering opportunities to help the police through trust and partnership. In the interview with Professor Smith, he shared his observations of similar experiences with the Black Panther Party in Oakland, California who also chose to police their communities.

The solutions presented by the representative gang members and the acceptance of those solutions by one police leader in Baltimore Police Department demonstrated the strength of the community partnership. This leader chose to listen and then accepted help from the community he was sworn to protect, regardless of their gang affiliations. Each had the common goal of easing the violence in the community. The participants stated in their interviews with me that they knew the police were there to help but it was of utmost importance that our police build trust with their communities in order to "partner" with citizens and find solutions.

Another theme that appeared in all three of these interviews was the use of inciting or disparaging language by police officers. I do believe this is the exception rather than typical of our police officers. Yet, it was talked about in each interview.

Disparaging or inciting language from our police officers is divisive and unacceptable, no exception. Each interview illustrated at least one situation where a police officer used language intended to incite anger or aggression from those they contacted during a police incident. If the community member chose or chooses to act out, then the police officer can and usually does respond with use of force. Oftentimes, we see the final snapshot of the use of force and call it "justified," as the officer was stopping the threat rather than the full video of the precipitating event and use of inappropriate language that created the confrontation.

What is frightening is this behavior in our police community may incite or encourage aggression that could result in deadly consequences. There is no reason for a police officer to call a young black male "boy" or a Hispanic youth a "Spic," as illustrated by three of the interviewed participants. The language serves no purpose but to offer an opportunity to anger and create confrontation. Additionally, that language has now created inequity between the police officer and the individual contacted. Those police officers using inflammatory language generate distance between themselves and community members. There is a significant loss of humanity with this type of behavior.

The theme of confronting or questioning of the police officer was also consistent in all three interviews. Some of the interviewees shared that there were opportunities to tell the officer that the behavior of the officer or the contact was questionable. Usually the questioning of the authority of the police officer angered that officer. The police officer felt threatened, that his authority was challenged. Most of the participants shared that when they challenged the knowledge of the police officer or questioned the contact, the officer responded by threatening to arrest them or detain them.

Many police officers can intertwine their ego with their authority, which can create disastrous results. The identification with the police profession is incredibly powerful. We give the ultimate authority to these men and women as police officers, entrusting them to protect citizens. To have citizens then question that authority usually creates anger; but underlying that anger is potentially fear and confusion. Perhaps there is a feeling of insecurity or loss of control and, therefore, authority. Again, I have experienced those individuals challenging or questioning my authority as a police officer. It can be very uncomfortable, yet it provides great opportunity to learn and grow rather than resent and hate.

What is important for police officers to remember is our community members do have a right to question our authority. This does not mean challenge or interfere with that authority as that has its own consequences. Opportunities to challenge a police officer can and should be done when the ability to do so offers safety for all involved in the incident. Our citizens have the right to question authority and they have the responsibility to comply with a direct order or command.

The questioning of authority does not mean the individual is threatening the officer. Consider when one's freedom is being restricted or taken away, would not most people ask why? What is most important is the police officer should know the answers when the community asks "why." If that officer does not know the answer, then find it.

One of the most powerful skills we have as police officers is the ability to listen to the community. For example, as a street officer the typical behavior is telling or directing the community to do something. As an investigator or detective there is a shift and it becomes important to listen to those community members. Solutions to investigations and crimes often come from simply listening to the community member. This was illustrated in Baltimore by the enlistment of gang members to help disperse crowds during a significant time of unrest and violence. There is a common ground between police and community, a partnership towards the same goal of peace and nonviolence, no matter the role of the participant.

The final theme that emerged was the desire to "know" the police officer. I found this theme so appealing in a time with such conflict. Here these individuals were asking to know those police officers as a solution to the conflict between police and community. Barry Graves said he wanted to know the police officer behind the badge, whether the officer had a family and what church that officer may attend. Professor Smith said he wanted the officer to know his name as well as him knowing the police officer's name.

Their suggestion of getting to know our police officers is imperative. If we can integrate our police officers into the communities they serve, there is a return to seeing each other as human beings rather than prey versus predator or suspect versus cop. The separatism of how we have policed our communities does not help us heal the fracture between police and community.

One of the interesting results of this solution is the ability to build trust between community and police. Currently, many in our marginalized communities have no reason to share important information with police officers. For example, in areas of high crime and gang activity community members might be hesitant to help the police solve crime, perhaps even when it would benefit them to share that information. The lack of trust furthers the divide between cops and citizens, with police officers feeling apathy and frustration for attempting to help the community.

Yet, if our police officers can begin to get to know our citizens then the healing may begin. While the suggested solution is simple, the effort will be significant. In picturing how this gets done, I do not see community stations as the solution. The solution is being in the community, beyond the building walls, beyond the patrol cars. This means we break down the boundaries that surround the police community. It entails police officers and police leaders immersed in the community and asking the questions that will allow that police officer to understand how the citizen wants to be policed.

Additionally, this type of police involvement builds a partnership with the community. As trust builds between citizen and police, this partnership provides police with additional resources to help prevent and solve crime in the community. For example, the recent incidents of mass shootings involving terrorism have necessitated community members speaking up when they have observed something unusual. If a community does not trust its police then there will not be any sharing of information and the community becomes unsafe. Yet, if there is trust between police and community then the members will feel safe to share that information, which thereby increases safety of all citizens. All members are working together to create safe and healthy communities.

CHAPTER 8

Solutions for Our Police Community

*"We cannot solve our problems with the same
thinking we used when we created them"*
Albert Einstein

Individual & Systemic Reformation

Maslow (1968) described in his *Hierarchy of Needs* the significant importance of meaning and purpose in our lives. This level of achievement in our development rises above physiological needs, safety concerns, and belonging-ness. To have a sense of service in police work provides a strong sense of meaning and purpose. In our research with police officers, the percentage of officers believing their work was a calling or a way to serve was over 90 percent. Their concept of service centered on wanting to do something that lifts them and enables them to bring their highest selves to their work.

Yet, police work can be as seductive as a mistress. It can consume an officer with the allure of excitement and power. The work can provide an officer the chance to become "larger than the self." The police persona can be powerful, focusing on self-importance, authority, and feelings of superiority. That officer can abuse the power that is given with the position and may become one of the problems in the organization or culture.

A systemic change in policing begins with an acknowledgement of personal responsibility, empathy, discipline, and compassion. What could the world look like with this intention? This section of individual solutions requires much self-reflection. Many of our police officers have shut off this ability to look within and actually see what their work means to them and the toll it has taken. Their work becomes mechanistic. Their hearts are walled off to stop the pain and hurt from infiltrating their soul. The many calls for service involving human destructiveness and suffering require them to compartmentalize their emotions and feelings.

Many of our police officers have shared they have experienced an increase in anger. With the inability to express emotion in a healthy way, the individual may become very dysfunctional. Those emotions ignored or "stuffed" may lead to the development of poor coping mechanisms that only foster the officer's isolation from healthy relationships with others. There can be an increase in divorce rates, disruptive behavior at work, and/or an increase in sick and injury leave. While I do not have any statistical data regarding this behavior in the United States, Liddell's study (2013) demonstrated the tremendous effects of stress on the UK's police forces with police officers off sick for three or more months and the costs of stress, PTSD and Burnout in UK forces at £99 million.

Anectodally, many police officers have shared their difficulties with maintaining resiliency if they have nothing beyond their job. Their identity of being a police officer is so powerful that it has consumed them and left them with no other identity. They leave their job, go home to their family, interrogate their loved ones, and completely check out from any involvement in familial relationships. Many officers report similar experiences and are aware of the dysfunctional nature of their behavior and that they do not want to be that way. It is time to provide education and training to help "innoculate" these police officers against the significant stress and trauma in their work.

Police officers recognize that the population around them does not understand the type of calls that are "typical." For example, I have made the mistake of talking about some of my own experiences in law enforcement only to recognize the looks of horror on the faces of those who asked the question about what it was like to be a police officer. The sharing of a story in my police career entails graphic images that most of the population was not ready to hear.

Our confrontation with evil and horror becomes commonplace, similar to what the military encounters. There are many moments of boredom in police work and then sudden snapshots of terror, ugliness, and destruction. Both ends of this spectrum create an opening for unethical behavior, corruption, and despair. The experiences of death and destruction offer police officers the opportunity to succumb to the horror or shut down feelings and emotions. Many times officers shut down quickly to cope. However, there is always the opportunity to share the experience and shed the emotion of that experience, moving one toward positive growth and change. Our abilities to share and teach each other in the police community can offer a tremendous opportunity for healing.

Sometimes, law enforcement may view these ugly experiences as a rite of passage, wanting to expose other officers to the destruction. For example, I remember when I left my first police department after working there ten years and was hired by another police agency in the Denver, Colorado metro area. Even though I had been a police officer/police sergeant at my first agency, I started over and was back in patrol. However, my new peers did not know or care about my prior experiences. One evening I was dispatched to a call of an unattended death. I was asked to take photographs of the scene and the victim. It was a gruesome scene and I quickly realized that I was being tested to see if I could handle the horror.

The call involved a man who had died in his apartment and his dog who had eaten part of the man's face. I took pictures and even made a joke or two as I did so. During the investigation of the scene, I remember one of the field-training officers calling for another training officer to bring his new recruit over to the scene. I then watched the training officers and their charges parade through the scene. The training officers were watching the faces of the new recruits, looking for any signs of weakness or distress. One trainee looked at the scene and did not demonstrate any emotion. The other trainee walked in after the first and I can still hear the gasp as he looked at the victim on the floor of his apartment. His shock at what he had just seen was so apparent.

Both trainees finished their training programs and went on to become excellent police officers. However, at what expense? What was the effect of the scene on each police officer? For that matter, what was the effect on all of us? Those scenes are still vivid in my memory but no emotion surrounds the picture. So, many police officers have similar experiences and those experiences take their toll unless we are wise enough to open our hearts and look at the effects of our profession, to ground ourselves in what we consider sacred beyond ourselves, something larger than the self and then use each experience to grow and mature.

What has happened in our police communities and in our military is a huge disservice to the emotional, social, physical, and spiritual wellbeing of our first responders and service personnel. This may become "undiagnosed trauma" in our officers and military. However, many of our communities have similar "undiagnosed trauma" from high levels of violence and crime. This is why it is so important to "fix" this problem in our police communities.

So, how do we fix this in our police community? I am a believer that we can teach police officers to be ethical, conscientious, and reflective. In a recent article in the Washington Post (2015), the authors were citing the changes to Las Vegas Police Department's use-of-force policy. In the policy's language, it states the importance of "the sanctity of human life." That powerful change in their policy resulted in a reduction in officer-involved shootings by half in 2013. So the language we use can be a huge predictor of our success or failure when exploring solutions.

In our law enforcement agencies, field-training officers are a critical component in teaching and training our police officers.

Field-training officers provide the greatest source of education and must be ethical and reflective as well. They must provide a positive example for the recruit. If the police recruit enters the profession with a training officer who does not care or is unethical, we can only expect to have that new officer adopt the trainer's behavior. Consequently, if our police trainers are positive, well trained, educated, and disciplined, there is a far better chance that the new officer will be ethical and conscientious.

Now, looking upwards in the organization we have to have police leaders and executives who are thinking and behaving ethically, reflectively, and conscientiously. Many of us are much better at looking at other people and their behavior rather than our own. But it is imperative that the police leaders and executives examine their own behavior, provide a culture of support for their police officers, and attempt to eliminate the opportunity for corruption. However, many police leaders and executives fail to understand the importance of examining their own behavior. It is very easy for a police executive to order his or her troops to change behavior but then fail to look inward at how that executive's behavior affects the culture and organization. So individual reformation must be initiated and supported by each member in the organization, top to bottom.

Zimbardo (2007, 2008) writes that not all is lost, that we are not doomed to become evil. Rather, it is important to "grow heroes" in society, by demonstrating the power of staying the course of one's moral compass and resisting the allure of the social conformity and obedience. This is possible for our individual police officers. Many of our law enforcement officers are doing this currently. However, is this a possibility from a systemic perspective? I believe it is possible to systemically change the police community. Through individual commitment, each member in that organization and the culture begin to change. It requires commitment + responsibility + accountability = Systemic Change

Toward Resilience

There has been an increasing amount of research and focus in the area of resilience. Exploring how our police officers cope with their work can help identify potential solutions to build resilience in our police officers. Do they seek unhealthy coping strategies that leave them broken, angry, and ill? "Feelings of hopelessness, fear, blame, pain, discomfort, vulnerability, and disconnection sabotage resilience" (Brown, 2010, p 73). Or do they find ways to stay engaged in their lives, maintain healthy relationships with others outside of police work, and function in healthy ways that build inner strength and health. The research we have done in the police community for the last decade has shown the majority of police officers are very resilient in their work:

> *and demonstrate high levels of self-control, compassion, professionalism and love for the work they have chosen to do. Their dedication to service is for many inspiring, revealing some of the noblest acts of self-sacrifice and altruism. These officers appear to have an ability to transform negative experiences, redirect their emotionally charged frustrations and move from feelings of victimization to using the experience to create new meaning and compassion.* (Smith & Charles, 2010, p 321)

What is critical to understand regarding this research is we do not teach our police officers how to become resilient. We teach our police to enforce the laws of the state and country. We train them to use force, to shoot, to drive, but we do not teach them how to survive emotionally and spiritually in their work. The topic of resilience is not presented in an academy but rather police officers may become unconsciously competent on how to maintain resiliency in their lives. In other words, these police officers cannot tell you how they learned to be resilient; they just are resilient.

Some police officers may not remain resilient, may lose faith in humanity, and become angry and cynical. So how do we help the police community maintain their resilience with the amount of responsibility, power, and authority that is given them? Not many jobs or professions have such an immediate influence on another human being's life. It is my belief that we educate our police community about the effects of their work, how to moderate work stressors, and offer techniques to help build resilience in our police officers.

Police officers learn to quickly master high levels of stress and control their emotions. We have failed our police officers by not providing significant training in stress management and resilience. Additionally, our police leaders and executives do not "check in" with our police officers. Our police executives often fail to demonstrate a caring organization that fosters employee value and simply assume our police officers are trained and can, therefore, master any situation.

Nevertheless, police officers can be "broken" by the repeated and unresolved or undisclosed trauma. Or police officers may lose direction and their moral compass. During the last decade of policing, there has been an introduction of debriefing counseling and peer support groups. Yet, many police officers still choose to suffer in silence rather than admit vulnerability. However, police supervisors and leaders who care for their employees should be more capable in recognizing distress in employee behavior.

There is recent research in resilience illustrating that resilience is created through the experience of the trauma. In a study of police constables, they were followed for twelve months of their career, from entry in the police profession. The results showed the police constables did benefit from the exposure to traumatic events (Burke & Shakespeare-Finch, 2011). Other studies demonstrate that first responders are more likely to succeed and find their work meaningful if they assumed personal responsibility for their responses to the trauma (Bartone, et al., 2008; Clohessy & Ehlers, 1999; Maytum, et al., 2004; McGee, 2006).

How do we find the work meaningful? Perhaps a better question is how do we keep police work meaningful? There is research that focuses on spirituality in the workplace that demonstrates the importance of growth and maturity, the significance of being "other-centered" versus "self-centered" (Maslow, 1968; Carlier, 1999; Smith & Charles, 2010). It is interesting that many police officers are very aware they present themselves as "self-centered" versus "other-centered," and their selfish nature. Perhaps this is a step toward self-reflection.

In one recent study we conducted (Charles, et al., 2014), we interviewed eleven police officers from several different police agencies in Colorado and then followed these police officers over the last three to five years of their careers. During that time, almost all of the participants suffered some type of major stressor or trauma to include: addiction, divorce, internal investigation, and work trauma. All of the police officers were able to recover from their hardship and regain balance and perspective. Their resilience helped them "bounce back" from difficult adversity.

These officers shared that during their challenge or trauma, it was imperative for them to work with their police supervisor and communicate with that supervisor rather than isolating themselves. Because of the perception of a team effort, they felt that there was support and resources provided to help them regain balance. Each of these officers were self-reflective and showed high levels of humility and introspection.

Meaningful questions for Resilience Practice
1.What would it take for you to "thrive" in your career?
2. Can you identify when you began to struggle with …
(Alcohol, Anger, Depression, Organizational Issues)?
3.When have you felt alone/abandoned in your police work/service?
4. Are you hurting or angry and don't know what to do about it?
5. Are you disconnected from: Self, Spiritual, Family, Friends, Career?

Integrity

This section is perhaps one of the most important chapters in "righting the ship" in our police communities. Entering the profession of police work is not an easy decision; for the police officer or the organization hiring the officer. Each must determine whether it is a good match.

Most police officers, whether they will admit it or not, enter into police work as a path towards helping others. A fraction of police applicants choose to enter police work as a way of achieving power. Those that enter for reasons of power "typically" do not last very long in the profession. Hopefully, good screening efforts remove these types of applicants. However, should a power hungry police cadet enter the profession and make it through training, he or she will not find the satisfaction with the work of a police officer.

Police officers who are seeking power will quickly reveal their true intentions. If the police culture matches the intention, either a grouping of police officers or a sector or district, then that police officer may survive in that culture and even thrive for several years. One example shared earlier was in New York Police Department's 75th precinct where corruption and brutality continued unchecked for approximately ten years.

Because this type of behavior is contradictory to the concept of service, their actions demonstrate their intentions and they can be easily identified if the police culture is focused on humanistic police service. The issue becomes whether those police leaders act upon those intentions or allow the corrupt behavior to continue. Power sought through police work may appear by gaining status, abusing people or peers, or corruption. The police culture must have high integrity and accountability in order to encourage easy identification.

What is unfortunate is when a police culture is more "accepting" of the unethical behavior. This happens very quickly when an organization fails to discipline its officers, chooses to ignore or excuse corrupt behaviors, or simply engages in similar corrupt behavior as illustrated in the Stanford Prison Experiment, Abu Ghraib, and the Clinton Correctional Facility. This is not just in our police communities. This possibility exists in any grouping of individuals.

The failure to discipline in police organizations occurs in almost any community. In a CNN report, New York Police Department often failed to discipline officers who used excessive force. A Citizen Complaint Review Board received 207 allegations of excessive force between 2010-2014. Ninety-two of those allegations were substantiated but the department gave minimal or no discipline to the officers approximately 67 percent of the time. In 66 percent of those cases where there was physical force, 15 percent were "officer-escalated situations" (CNN, 2014). The report recommended "de-escalation" techniques or slowing down the interaction of the situation to increase the amount of time an officer has to think through a situation rather than react.

In my many years as a police supervisor, I have experienced and observed similar inconsistencies regarding attempts to discipline officers. I have also witnessed when agencies have chosen to ignore or excuse bad behavior in their police officers. That behavior always returns and is usually more pronounced. Quickly, there is a new culture of behavior established. Further, if the officer's disciplinary process extends for a lengthy period of time, the unethical or bad behavior may simply go underground where it is not noticed by supervisors. As time passes, the effects of the bad behavior may tend to be less impactful than when it was first observed. In other words, the shock is over and the agency attempts to return to "normal" or the members of the organization become worn down by the length of the disciplinary process.

From a psychological perspective, when addressing behavior we know that if we want to deter negative behavior there needs to be swift punishment. Otherwise, the individual is reinforced to continue the bad behavior. In order to change behavior, there must be consequences for bad behavior. Whether training puppies, rearing children, or developing good police officers, our abilities to discipline for good behavior is paramount in developing good behavior. Choosing to ignore or to minimize bad behavior simply encourages that behavior. In fact, the bad behavior will usually increase as the individual seeks to find a boundary to bounce against. The established boundaries in an organization, family, or society help individuals determine where they begin and end and are important in self-identification.

While the behavior I observed as a police supervisor was relatively minor in comparison to some of the other agencies in the United States, any unethical behavior destroys the trust between the police organization and its members. As corruption or unethical behavior then collides with the community members, the trust is then further damaged between police and community. The behavior I originally observed and attempted to correct did resurface with increased intensity, with the agency losing several members to integrity issues. Other members involved in the corruption certainly damaged their careers as well.

In Ferguson, Missouri, the Justice Department released a report after the Michael Brown shooting that described the police department had a "tendency to use unnecessary force against vulnerable groups." So the fatal event between Michael Brown and Officer Wilson brought to the surface the underlying issues between police and community. The culture of the organization demonstrated a clear disparity between community members of color and the rest of the community.

During an event at a community college in Modesto, California concerning policing and people of color, two police leaders from the local law enforcement agencies attended to speak with the audience about recent issues between police and community. After watching the film *Black in America Black and Blue,* one police leader told the audience that he was shocked by the actions of the police in New York as portrayed in the film. He made a blanket statement to the audience that policing in California is not the same as it is on the east coast and that behavior would not be tolerated in his organization. Some members of the audience were very upset and shared their voices of disagreement. Unfortunately, this is a mistake many police executives make when addressing the public about sensitive issues.

Police leaders cannot afford to make blanket statements about police behavior. It is imperative for police leaders/executives to understand it is time to look within our police cultures. I would guarantee there is at least one police officer in the organization who is operating unethically. There is at least one police officer who has violated someone's rights, abused someone (verbally or physically), or done something unethical. We cannot state that the behavior illustrated in New York Police Department would never happen in a California police organization or any other police organization. So, it is imperative to look within, to evaluate what our culture truly is, to honestly question whether we are "allowing" unethical behavior, or ignoring the signs of hidden corruption.

When we choose a life of police service, we choose to share the deepest good of our souls and hearts. When we fail to care for ourselves, we may break from our grounding that keeps us human. It becomes easy to react like an animal, predator to prey. One police officer reflected the importance of compassion in his work, "You want to put the bad guys away, you want to help people be accountable, you want to let that other person know that I'm not going to let these people pick on you" (Charles, 2005, p111). Another officer shared, "So we're connected. It doesn't matter what culture it is, we're connected somehow" (Charles, 2005, p112). These police officer illustrate the importance of connecting their police work to compassion. For them, their police work became a service that incorporated the themes of humanism, other-centered, and a sense of being "called" to police work.

In my research, many of the participants described the importance of their integrity:

One participant reflected on the importance of spiritual integrity:

> *I think the most important thing you bring to the job is your ethics and your character. I just think it's in your heart and you've got to have a moral compass that just always points in the right direction no matter how bad the seas are around you. The compass has got to be always true and you either have it or you don't. You've got to dedicate yourself to it and you've got to have sound moral principles.* (Charles, 2005)

Another participant believed in the importance of spirituality and morality for police work:

> *Some people are into that uniform and that power thing and if you don't have your spirituality and morality, you kind of go the fast road because it's so easy. We have a lot of crime and deal with a lot of bad folks. If you're not a Christian or if you don't have something grounding you, you can get lost in it, kind of like a relative morality.*
> (Charles, 2005)

Awaken the Spiritual Warrior

In the research we have done in the United States and the United Kingdom with the police community, the police officers interviewed provided rich examples of how important their spirituality was to their work, their health, and survival beyond the stress and trauma incurred in policing. Three common themes emerged in over 150 interviews: 1) spiritual philosophies and practices, including the belief in something greater than self that "calls" the participants to police work; 2) the importance of human relationships in supporting a humanistic approach to service; and 3) spiritual responses to the experiences of human destructiveness, suffering, evil, and death (Charles, 2005; Charles, 2009; Smith & Charles, 2010).

Fry (2003) wrote that workplace spirituality enhances the employee's joy, peace, job satisfaction, and commitment. The research we have conducted over the last decade has shown an overwhelming agreement that police officers believe they were "called" to the profession. The meaning and purpose of being a protector of society was paramount (Charles, 2009; Smith & Charles, 2010; Charles, et al., 2014)

Police officers learning to incorporate their spirituality into their police work was not taught nor trained. This is simply inherent in the officer and was not dependent on whether the police organization supported them. In fact, many of our participants shared that they did not believe they were supported by their police leaders or police organizations. In Liddell's (2013) survey, 79 percent of the respondents did not feel supported by the police organization.

What is interesting is the type of police work done by these police officers reflects a connection with community members, high levels of integrity, and humanism. It is a puzzle why a police leader would not support officers in their approach. However, in order to bring this type of support into our police organizations, our police leaders need to be self-aware, secure, and open to addressing all questionable issues within the organization. These police executives would then build a framework of organizational values that reflect the police officer's humanistic and service approach. Values such as: Trust, humility, tolerance, and compassion for all members of the organization would be weaved in the very fabric of the organizational framework (Giacalone, 2003).

The shift in workplace culture could inspire its members to experience transcendence through their work, feel connected to community, and allow for the expression of compassion and service in their work. These police leaders would then walk with their members, mentoring and encouraging, disciplining and educating, and demonstrating trust. This would demand that our police leaders have insight and humility in order to evaluate their organizations and culture, as well as themselves.

When police officers incorporate their spirituality into their police work, they appear to be able to innoculate themselves from the effects of the stress and trauma. Many of the participants interviewed were followed over several years. Their work remained meaningful and purposeful. Some experienced difficulties at work or in their personal life but were able to recover and find their way back on track. They had established powerful and positive social support. They chose friends from outside the police profession to provide diversity in their world.

By comparison, there were police officers that lost faith in what they believed was sacred: Humanity, Truth, Family, Religion,

Compassion, Ethics, Values. Through crisis or confrontation with trauma and human suffering, they were not able to assimilate the experiences and move past the trauma. Those experiences weighed heavy on those police officers who were afflicted with depression, struggles with ego, and anger. They quickly became detached from the sense of service and saw the profession as just a job. They lost meaning and purpose. Their purpose became a financial pursuit and these officers usually worked several hours of overtime during the week. These police officers expressed no incorporation of spirituality in their police work. The work appeared to become far less enjoyable.

When exploring how to keep our police officers healthy and thriving, the incorporation of a police officer's spirituality appears to provide a tremendous source of coping mechanisms, resiliency, and higher level thinking for problem solving. However, these results encourage more research in the police community in order to identify additional resources to promote a healthy police community.

<u>*Questions for the Spiritual Warrior*</u>
1. What do you consider sacred, larger than self?
2. How do you align with that sacredness?
3. How do you cope with human destructiveness and suffering?
4. What support mechanisms do you have?

Mentoring

Writing this book has been a gift. Sometimes that gift has been like the ridiculous fruitcake you get and think, "how soon can I throw this thing out." Sometimes the writing is a precious offering, where I am overwhelmed by it. Nonetheless the gift is honored and respected.

One night I woke up from a dream. I had taken a break from my writing. In this dream, I was working with two young ladies, who were Hispanic. They were upset because we had to clean some bathroom stalls. I was attempting to share with them the importance of the work, to have a clean bathroom stall was wonderful. Both girls were not buying my perspective, complaining that the bathrooms just get dirty again. I told the girls that the stalls do get dirty, yet we are always needing to continue house cleaning.

At some point in the dream, the bathroom area was then an outside view. An old Volkswagon van, orange colored body with a white roof slowly drove by. Inside the van were two young black men in the front seats and two young Hispanic or black young women sitting in the back seats. They were staring as they drove by and I turned to ask if they needed something. The driver said they were just slowing down to make sure everything was okay with the two young girls I was working with in the bathroom stalls.

I realized the vehicle occupants had identified me as a cop. But, I was not in uniform, nor had I ever been identified as a cop in the dream until this moment. I told the young men that it was good that they were checking to make sure all was okay. The young men and women seemed a bit stunned by my casualness about their vigilance. Then the young driver said, "We are on donut patrol." I made a gesture to them as if I was belly laughing, taking my hands and bouncing them in front of my stomach. They looked at me and smiled and drove off.

I woke up stunned by this dream. First, why the bathrooms in the dream? They represented a dirty or disgusting environment that needed cleaning? Could I equate that to the issues facing us in the police community and the conflict with our communities? Second, why was I suddenly identified as a cop in the dream? I have been retired from police work since April 2013 and have not had one police dream since that time. Yet, I was a cop and not in uniform and these young people knew I was a cop. The scene of the young people driving slowing by and checking on my behavior with the young females appears to me to be reflective of community members checking on how police are treating their citizens. My response was an agreement and understanding about them checking on the girls. I understood in the dream that I needed to build trust.

In reflecting on my dream, I believe it is paramount that we all keep an eye on each other. That is our responsibility as community members to take care of those around us. It is not just a law enforcement goal. It is the goal of all individuals living together on this planet. My dream response to the young people was to agree with their involvement or watchful approach. Their dream response was slight surprise and then acceptance. Any potential issue or pending problem evaporated with our responses in this dream. I am left wondering about the simplicity of this dream.

The dream I experienced feels as if I have been mentored by someone, perhaps those who have been interviewed in the book. Almost all of those individuals interviewed talked about how important it was for someone to teach them how to talk to "white people." To hear this from these brave interviewees was difficult. I am one of those "white people."

Yet, each of these individuals offered the concept of mentoring as a solution. This concept was not offered as a solution but rather illustrated through their stories about the importance of mentoring. If it was so important for these people to be taught how to talk to "white people" and police officers, then why are we not looking at its importance for our police officers.

Law enforcement has had the concept of "mentoring" through its history, but rather informally. For example, police officers from east coast police agencies have referred to a mentor in their career as their "rabbi," as one who watches over them and helps advance their career as well as protects officers from any inequitable treatment. Some of the continued mentoring in police work involves the importance of field-training officers and their trainees. A field-training officer usually has a tremendous effect on a new police officer.

There are some formalized mentoring programs in our police communities across the United States. For example, the city of Fontana, California and the Kent Police Department in Kent, Washington have structured mentoring programs for their new police officers to help those officers assimilate into the new culture (City of Kent, 2007). This is ancillary to the field-training program and is designed to improve retention. This is an excellent approach in caring for police employees and creating a positive and ethical culture.

When I think about my training officers, some were amazingly helpful and some were destructive. The great training officers in my career actually did help me, teaching me how to talk with people. However, the "people" in the first communities I served were mostly "white people." So the lessons were not far from where I was familiar.

As I matured as a police officer, I became a mentor for other police officers. I realized the importance of this role when I remember teaching new officers how to shine their boots, how to talk to someone in crisis and not provoke aggression, or how to make coffee for the next shift. This mentoring was powerful and important as it fostered success in the next generation of police officers. If I wanted to make sure that these new police officers could help me in a critical incident then it was important to train and mentor them with the highest intentions.

The concept of mentoring, in my experience, seemed to fade in its importance as I continued my career in police work. Training officers were pushed to the limit with new recruit after new trainee. They did not get any relief nor much support from police leaders. The goal was to get new police officers trained as quickly as possible; it was quantity over quality. There was no time to provide the observational learning necessary for a new police officer to watch and mimmick behavior that truly reflects good police work. Unfortunately, the use of structured mentoring programs in Fontana, California and Kent Police Department appear to be the exception to the rule in our police communities in the United States.

New police officers are turned out into the community without much life experience and limited applicable training. By applicable training, I am referring to communication and de-escalation techniques needed to communicate with community members in crisis. Training then becomes the responsibility of the community, a community who may be marginalized, who may not have been mentored by others, and who may suffer from "undisclosed trauma" themselves.

Can we not imagine confrontation, anger, aggression, and fear on both sides of the conflict?

The concept of "slowing down" our police officers is critical today with the confrontation of such strong emotions. This does not mean our police officers need to wait until they are assaulted. It means training our police personnel to think critically about the situation they encounter in order to problem solve rather than react like an animal. However, our police officers need positive examples, mentors, and coaches to teach them how to talk to their communities.

So the question I was left with after interviewing Barry Graves was: What if we develop mentors for our police community? Now the concept of these mentors in our police community would look noticeably different. These mentors would teach our police officers about their community as they would be the community members. They would teach and mentor our police officers to understand the people they serve. They would be educated in the issues facing the community.

Some may argue that the time involved with these mentors would be extensive. However, the training of a police officer is extensive and intensive. We should be focused on training our officers to be most effective in how they do their work. We should be concerned about the training because if the training is effective and meaningful then the officer should feel more capable and confident. The work becomes meaningful and purposeful and the individual feels valued in police work, community, and the organization. So we can push these new police officers through but then the "on-the-job" training should incorporate a mentorship into the community and the work.

For example, Police Commissioner Bratton admittedly stated their deployment of new police officers into high crime areas was a mistake. These new police officers did not know the job, which allowed many errors by these officers. Former LAPD Police Chief, Daryl Gates, also accepted responsibility for his police agency's failure to assimilate new police members as they were hired. Unfortunately, these mistakes can be deadly for the new officers and the community members. If the mistakes are not deadly, they may leave permanent scars on the officer and the community members. We cannot afford to take these chances anymore. Post-traumatic stress, suicide, addiction issues, and "undisclosed trauma" linger in the police community and in those they serve when these mistakes are made by our police leaders and organizations.

Therefore, mentors in our police community could look powerfully engaging. For example, we could assign retired police officers to some of our new police officers to educate about humility, the power of an ethical reputation, and how to best thrive in the job. Another example of mentoring could be an internship with various youths engaged in or having participated in low level crimes or nuisance crimes. These youths could teach the new police officer about how to work with this type of juvenile behavior, answer questions about how to best approach them, what words incite anger or frustration, and how to partner with them rather than alienate them.

Mentors could come from any segment of our population. Even the "criminal" population could become involved in mentoring new police officers. Obviously, these individuals would be screened to determine whether they could do the work or whether their involvement would be detrimental. However, there are many individuals who have committed non-violent crimes, even felonies, that would and could offer help. Perhaps an individual who has committed some type of fraud and wants to make amends for those crimes has decided to mentor an officer in looking for criminal behavior. That individual could teach the best ways to approach those individuals committing property crimes. In fact, nominal fees for their service could provide value to both the officer and the "mentor" in the partnership. Each would understand where the other comes from in the mentorship. The police officer and the "mentor" have the opportunity to learn from each other.

Just as many African Americans have had to learn how to talk to white people, police must learn to talk to community members. A "mentoring" program that integrates our community members provides our police officers a better understanding of those in the community. If that community is a marginalized community then the mentor offers the police officer valuable insight about what that feels like for the community. The police officer has the opportunity to empathize where the citizen has been and then build a partnership with the community mentor.

For example, it is difficult for a white person to understand that the presence of a police officer to a young black male creates fear for that young male. That young male has not engaged in any criminal activity but just the presence of the police officer means he must be careful about his movements, his actions are controlled, he is not free. For the white person, there is freedom because the police officer is there to protect that person. He or she is free to move about without concern. Our police officers that work with marginalized communities must begin to understand and stand in that perspective. The ability to do so offers that police officer a significant opportunity to police from the heart, to serve with compassion and empathy, to empower and engage with that community.

In fact, we have come full circle and back to integration: Integration of our police officers into communities. I can envision meals being shared with the police officer and the mentor and the mentor's family and friends. Certainly, there are times when mentors could not work with police officers. Police work is unpredictable and can go from boring to violent in seconds. However, the mentorship could take place on training days or during specific times or meetings. The amount of time with the mentor would not have to be time consuming but rather meaningful exchange of information between police officer and mentor.

For example, a new police officer spending time with a young black male and the exchange of where that young man lives and how he lives would be powerful and meaningful. Instead of that young male being pulled over by officer after officer, sometimes hundreds of times, that young man gives valuable information about how he is made to feel with the excessive contact. The new police officer can share his thoughts about why the young man is getting stopped. The communication between police officer and community members would build understanding, compassion, and growth that would change each individual at a cellular level.

Again, police work is dangerous and violent at times and there are moments on a shift or during the week where this type of communication could not happen. But there is always time at some point to have this type of mentoring for our police officers. The "community-mentoring program" could offer nominal income for the "mentor" or the program could solicit volunteers. Students could intern or those interested in a future career in police work could volunteer. Community members could be enlisted for their valuable knowledge for a stipend or salary.

The innumerable types of mentors for our police officers could afford a well-rounded experience based knowledge about how to police our communities. A new police officer mentored in homelessness from a woman who has been there gains new insight about how to talk with someone who has just crawled out of a dumpster looking for scrap metal to sell. A young juvenile who is a skateboarder, has been bullied by others, and is angry can mentor a new officer about why the language a "cop" may use can create such anger that the juvenile just wants to strike out. A young Hispanic or African American can mentor that police officer so that officer can know how a police officer's behavior can agitate men and women from another ethnicity.

When we look at the possibilities of this type of mentoring, there are positives and negatives. Some of the negatives may be the mentor may not be a good fit for the police organization. For example, the criminal background may be too extensive or may risk the security of information. However, the positives are numerous. For instance, police officers could become actively engaged in their communities they serve.

If the police officers and police leaders are open to the information given and the mentorship provided, then their work can become less difficult because officers are not constantly engaged in a battle with the community. There is more understanding and knowledge about each other. We become integrated with each other and we are doing the work that we are supposed to be doing. We are returning those who fall below the line of civility and public order and gently returning them back to order.

It is very easy to separate from that which we do not understand or are not familiar with in our world. The sense of judgment creates separation and leads people to label something as "good" or "bad," different or wrong. Walls are then built to further the separation. What may follow is greed, keeping the "others" from what one has acquired, superiority in the belief that one is better than another, and finally violence.

This type of "separatism" behavior in our police communities makes the work so much more difficult in policing our communities. When we can see each other as equals, human beings on the same planet, each trying to make their way through life, we share common goals and values. We can lessen the separateness in our world by listening to each other, learning from another, and asking each other to know how best to treat the other.

Recently there have been acts of terrorism in our country. Regardless of where the terrorist came from, the community is such an important part of the solution in fighting terrorism. In an age of terrorism, it is imperative to engage our community members. If the public/community fails to trust law enforcement then we lose safety. By making those in our communities the enemy, we lose vital information. Our police leaders have been in the news pleading for our community members to pay attention to potential terroristic behavior, that we need to engage the community in the "fight" against terrorism. The citizens are demanding that the police leaders and officers engage with their communities. They have been asking for a long time. Now it is time for the police community to respond if we want the community's help.

CHAPTER 9

Conclusion

*"A person who does not take care of themselves
will not take care of others"*
Oprah Winfrey

The timing of this book is purposeful. The crisis that our police communities in the United States currently face is the direct result of antiquated behavior. Our police communities can choose to ignore the current issues facing them or decide to change their behavior and culture to meet the needs of all human beings. What I have written in these pages is a brief look at what is happening in our police communities. I offer explanations as to why this behavior is occurring. I have followed with potential solutions for individualistic and systemic changes in our police organizations.

It is my belief that the problems before us are so pronounced as to create a high level of chaos, which begs us to change. When we are faced with such stages of chaos, it becomes very uncomfortable until we struggle with our challenges and reach a higher degree of understanding. To ignore those struggles, to fail to address those challenges will only further the divide currently facing our police and marginalized communities. Our police communities are unique microcosms that provide rich and raw perspectives of what is going wrong and/or right in our society. Many of our citizens are struggling with inequities in our systems, with poverty and crime in our communities, with mental illness, and anxiety and depression.

However, many of our police officers are also suffering from similar issues. Both communities, the police and citizens, have struggled with feelings of isolation and loss of meaning and purpose. Many believe they are not valued in their work or communities. We have years of undisclosed trauma in our communities and police organizations and now they are both colliding into each other, with each side aggressively demonstrating that they have had enough. Each community, albeit police or marginalized, is insisting that the other change. Emotions are high with neither side wanting to back away.

Our marginalized communities have asked and now are demanding change. They are highlighting the abusive police behavior that is no longer acceptable. Currently, our police organizations have "reacted" to the conflict. Now it is time to slow our thinking down and look at our responses to the current conflicts in our communities.

This does not mean the act of hesitation. I am not suggesting that our police officers hesitate before taking action. I am stating firmly that our police communities engage their hearts and brains together to protect and serve, to protect human sanctity.

Yet, within our police communities, we have tens of thousands of police officers that are quietly and unassuming performing their jobs at the highest levels of service. Our research has shown those officers who feel "called" or "compelled" to work as a police officer, have a strong sense of humanistic service, and understand their role as a police officer are not taught this approach. Instead, these individuals become this type of police officer, either through their own moral compass or belief systems or having been mentored by another about the sacredness of all human life. These officers are our best solutions and examples of what can and will work because our communities are demanding that the police culture change.

The time of complete obedience to authority, extreme positions of power and control, and exerting abusive behavior is over. Police must meet each member in our communities and actually see the humanity within that individual. We must work to make our police officers conscientious, empathetic, and responsible. Our training must reflect these same values. Our police organizations must incorporate those same values in their culture. This demands that we slow down our mental processes and begin to think in higher cognitive areas of our brain. We are not hunting prey and we are not the predator in a police uniform. We are safeguarding humanity, which means the drug addict that crawled out of the dumpster is just as important as the male in a three-piece suit when each needs a police officer. We do not get to choose who we serve.

Our responses to crisis require police officers slow down and respond rather than react. Our brains are magnificently capable of processing information at incredible speeds. By slowing down the thought process, the individual has an opportunity to process information in all areas of the brain. The thought process has the opportunity to reach the pre-frontal cortex or our higher functioning areas of the brain. Actually our brain and our responses become faster the more we learn to process information from our front lobes, our higher executive functioning (Charles, et al., 2014). Here, is where we can see other solutions, we can problem-solve, and we can find empathy and compassion.

For example, during my tenure as a police officer I have experienced many situations where I was justified to shoot someone. I could have just pulled the trigger. I remember one call to a convenience store where a female driver was acting out and the store clerk called to have the police check on her. I contacted this female as she sat in her car. She had a small child in the backseat. The female was distraught and crying.

I was the only police officer on duty at the time of this call and it was my responsibility to handle the scene. She tried to leave instead of continuing to talk with me. I made a critical error and reached inside the car. She quickly began to back up the car with me hanging on the driver's side of the vehicle. I was scared and knew I may have to shoot her before she got on the road and continued to drag me. However, I knew she was scared and upset. I decided to talk to her. As she backed up, I said, "Please stop. If you don't stop, you are going to kill me so please stop." I could have shot her, I could have "stopped the threat," but chose not to shoot and she stopped.

Had I viewed her as a threat, less than human, or myself as superior, it would have been easier to shoot her. I would not have cared or been concerned about her. I am confident that there are hundreds of thousands of experiences where our police officers have chosen not to shoot when justified to do so. This does not mean our police officers should never shoot when confronted with lethal force or a deadly assault. Instead, it is a call to remain mentally and emotionally flexible, to remain open to possible solutions, to think in the higher cognitive functioning areas of our brains. When we close down emotionally or mentally, when we are angry or stressed, when we experience high levels of fear then we close down and limit our abilities to think clearly.

Our mid brain is like our animal brain. This part of our brain can quickly take over and run our emotions, actions, and our higher thinking processes. Our highest level of thinking shuts down just like a computer going off-line. The situation in front of us becomes prey versus predator rather than problem-solver. Our limbic system in this mid brain is not wired for hope, happiness, or compassion. It is wired for fighting or fleeing from perceived dangers or threats. It is where anger, fear, and aggression reside.

Therefore, I am asking the police community to recommit to the ideals of the profession. There must be significant changes in training to reflect "the utmost importance of human sanctity." We must provide education to our police officers on how and why we must de-escalate and when it is important. This will further help our police officers slow down and think of alternate solutions. Finally, we must mentor our police officers, the organization, and the community. This commitment will then foster a sense of value in our police officers in our organizations.

This is the police pursuit of the common good, that we serve all members of a given community (Gibbons, 2015). Yes, we are mainly an individualistic society. However, our individual pursuits should not perpetuate abusive or mistreatment of another. That is the balance we must find between the individual and the common good. Let us shift our actions in the profession of policing. Perhaps the excitement of police work occurs when an officer has the chance to save a life. To be able to say, as a police officer, that he or she changed a volatile situation and ended it peacefully can become the goal. What if we rewarded our officers for creative problem-solving and peaceful pursuits? Instead of idolizing the angry "warrior" officer, let us see if we can help that officer find some peace and meaning in police work and heal the undisclosed trauma. It is there just below the surface of consciousness asking to be healed.

Currently, what may remain in the way are police executives and leaders. These suggestions can and will provide solutions to mend the conflict between our marginalized communities and our police officers. But nothing will come into being until there is complete commitment and participation from our police executives and leaders. This is not a patrol issue or an individual officer problem. This is a systemic issue and must be managed as such. It is not enough for our police leaders to "sign off" on the training and education and then fail to participate. It is imperative that our complete police system and culture commit to change. Otherwise, the efforts may be in vain, limited in their approach, and probably a waste of time.

The solutions presented in this book provide the police community with a potential course to follow. The participants interviewed in the book have given their perspective about how they want to be policed. They have offered that they want to know the men and women who are protecting them. They want those police officers to know their community. To be a cop is to also be a human being. It should be our goal to be a full personality in balance with our work.

The next stage for police work is the acknowledgement and connection to our communities and each other. Our ability to connect and re-engage with each other provides us with an increase in the meaning and purpose in our work. We must strengthen authentic power, connection, healing, humanism, safety, and balance. It is the Pursuit of the Common Good.

> *The experience of authentic power is "when we align our thoughts, emotions, and actions with the highest part of ourselves, we are filled with enthusiasm, purpose, and meaning. Life is rich and full. We have no memory of fear. Are joyously and intimately engaged with our world* (Zukav, 1989)

I have faith that what I have written in this book is pertinent to helping our police communities. I am basing this on 27 years of experience as a sworn police officer. I am backing my observations with education and experience as a research psychologist, having observed human behavior for years, researched that behavior, and written on those observations. If you are challenged by what is written in these pages, I ask you to remain open as I did when "schooled" on how we should be policing in the United States. I do not mind conflict. Conflict can usually take us to a higher level of understanding as long as the main goal is not to win. You can be angry but use that anger to explore what needs to change in our police community.

When you think of condemning what is written here, think whether you are without any fault or flaw. I have made mistakes. I have attempted to share some of those mistakes with you. Our mistakes offer valuable lessons to improve, to show others how to do it better. I am hoping these words help to mentor our new generation of police officers, those compassionate in their service, intending to educate and enforce our communities with the highest of ideals.

This is my duty to help our police communities re-engage with our marginalized communities. Let us look at our behavior, recognize our mistakes, change that behavior, and change our community. Our morality is very fragile. Therefore our highest levels of thinking and believing must guard it. It cannot be allowed to break under the weight of evil, misconduct, and abuse. By recommitting to our main values and goals of police service, we lose nothing and gain the opportunity to feel connected to our work. This is not about blame but rather our responsibility to protect and serve our communities. We must get this right. I leave our exploration with one last quote.

> *There is a principle, which is a bar against all information, which is proof against all arguments, and which cannot fail to keep a man in everlasting ignorance – that principle is contempt prior to investigation* William Paley.

BIBLIOGRAPHY

Adams, K., Alpert, G., Dunham, R., Garner, J., Greenfield, L., Henriquez, M., et al. (1999, November 1). *http://bjs.gov/index. cfm?ty=pbdetail&iid=809*. Retrieved January 12, 2015, from Bureau of Justice Statistics: www.bjs.gov

Alpert, G. P. (2004). *Understanding police use of force: Officers, suspects, and reciprocity.* New York, New York: Cambridge University Press.

Bartone, P., Roland, R., Picano, J., & Williams, T. (2008). Psychological happiness predicts success in U.S. Army Special Forces. *International Journal of Selection and Assessment, 16* (1), 78-81.

Berg, B. (1998). *Law enforcement: An introduction to police in society.* Boston: Allyn & Bacon.

Brown, B. (2010). *The gifts of imperfection: Letting go of who you think you're suppose to be and embrace who you are.* Center City, MN: Hazelden.

Burke, K., & Shakespeare-Finch, J. (2011). Markers of resilience in new police officers: Appraisal of potentially traumatizing events. *Traumatology.*

Carlier, I. (1999). Finding meaning in police traumas. In J. &. Violanti, *Police traumas: Psychological aftermath of civilian combat* (pp. 227-233). Springfield, Il: Charles C. Thomas.

Charles, G. (2005, August). How spirituality is incorporated in police work: A qualitative study. San Francisco, CA: Unpublished dissertation.

Charles, G. L. (2009). How spirituality is incorporated in law enforcement. *FBI Law Enforcement Bulletin, 78* (5).

Charles, G., Travis, F., & & Smith, J. (2014). Policing and spirituality: Their impact on brain integration and consciousness. *Journal of Management, Spirituality & Religion, 11* (3), 230-244.

City of Kent, W. (2007). *Police Mentoring Program.* Retrieved January 9, 2016, from kentwa.gov: http://kentwa.gov/content.aspx?id=9956

Clohessy, S., & Ehlers, A. (1999). PTSD symptoms, response to intrusive memories and coping in ambulance workers. *British Journal of Clinical Psychology, 38,* 251-263.

CNN (Director). (2015). *Black in America: Black and Blue* [Motion Picture].

CNN. (2014, August). NYPD fails to discipline officers who use excessive force, report says. New York, NY.

Diehl, M. &. (2010). Risk and resilience factors in coping with daily stress in adulthood: The role of age, self-concept incoherence, and personal control. *Developmental Psychology, 46,* 1132-1146.

Russell, T. (Director). (2015). *The Seven Five* [Motion Picture]. East New York, United States.

Figley, C. (1999). Police compassion fatigue (PCF): Theory, research, assessment, treatment, and prevention. In J. &. Violanti (Ed.), *Police trauma: Psychological aftermath of civilian combat* (pp. pp. 37-53). Springfield, IL, United States of America: Charles C Thomas.

FRONTLINE. (2001, February 27). *www.pbs.org*. Retrieved January 29, 2016, from Frontline: http://www.pbs.org/wgbh/pages/frontline/shows/lapd/interviews/gates.html

Fry, L. (2003). Toward a theory of spiritual leadership. *The leadership quarterly, 14*, 693-727.

Giacalone, R. A. (2003). Toward a science of workplace spirituality. In C. L. Jurkiewicz, *Handbook of workplace spirituality and organizational performance* (pp. 3-28). New York, NY: M. E. Sharp.

Gibbons, M. T. (Ed.). (2015). The Encyclopedia of Political Thought. New York, New York: John Wiley & Sons, Ltd.

Gilmartin, K. (2002). *Emotional survival for law enforcement: A guide for officers and their families.* E-S Press.

Implicit, P. (2011). *Project Implicit.* Retrieved November 7, 2015, from implicit.harvard.edu/implicit/: https://implicit.harvard.edu/implicit/

Kennedy, J. F. (1968, April 5). On the mindless menace of violence. Clevelamd, OH.

Kristian, B. (2014, July 2). Seven reasons police brutality is systemic, not anecdotal. *The American Conservative*.

LexisNexis. (2013). *Toronto Star Newspapers*. Retrieved from Crime Free Day in New York: www.lexisnexis.com

Liddell, E. (2013). Prevalence on PTSD, Compassion Fatigue and Burnout in the Emergency Services. *Presentation to the Police Federation Health and Safety Conference*. Police Federation Headquarters.

Maslow, A. (1968). *Towards a psychology of being*. New York, NY: D. Van Nostrand Co.

Maytum, J., Heiman, M., & Garwick, A. (2004). Fatigue and burnout in nurses who work with children with chronic condictions and their families. *Journal of Pediatric Health Care, 18*, 171-179.

McGee, E. (2006). The healing circle: Resiliency in nurses. *Issues in Mental Health Nursing, 27* (1), 43-51.

Millman, D. (1979). *The warrior athlete body mind & spirit: Self-transformation through total training*. Walpole, NH: Stillpoint Publishing.

Nietzsche, F. (1899). *Beyond good and evil*. Public Domain.

Powers, W. (2004). Managing the problem employee. *Poster session presented at Northwestern University Police Staff and Command School*. Centennial: Northwestern University.

Rich, S. &. (2015, December 26). *A year of reckoning: Police fatally shoot nearly 1,000*. Retrieved December 30, 2015, from www.washingtonpost.com/sf/investigative/2015/12/26/a-year-of-

reckoning-police-fatally-shoot-nearly-1000/: http://www.
washingtonpost.com

Serpico, F. (2014, October 23). Police are still out of control. *Law and
Order*.

Smith, J. & Charles, G. (2010). The revelance of spirituality in policing: A dual analysis. *International journal of police science and
management, 12* (3), 1-17.

Teel, R. (2014). *This life is joy: Discovering the spiritual laws to live more
powerfully, lovingly, and happily*. New York, NY: Penguin.

Violanti, J. (1999). Trauma in police work: A psychosocial model. In
J. Violanti, & D. Paton, *Police trauma: Psychological aftermath of
civilian combat*. Springfield, IL: Charles C. Thomas.

Wallace-Wells, B. (2015, November 30). *Baltimore After Freddy Gray:
A Laboratory of Urban Violence*. Retrieved December 1, 2015, from
nymag.com: http://nymag.com/daily/intelligencer/2015/11/
baltimore-after-freddie-gray-html

Waters, J. a. (2007). Police stress: History, contributing factors, symptoms, and interventions. . *Policing: An international journal of police strategies & management, 30* (2), 169-188.

Wickramasekera, I. E. (1988). *Clinical behavioral medicine: Some concepts and procedures*. New York, New York: Plenum Press.

Wikipedia. (n.d.). *WikipediA*. Retrieved October 3, 2015, from
WikipediA The Free Encyclopedia: www.wikipedia.org

Wilson, J., & Kelling, G. (1982, March). Broken windows. *The Atlantic
Monthly* .

Winfrey, O. (2015, October 14). (CBSN, Interviewer)

Zimbardo, P. (2008, September 23). *Psychology of evil.* Retrieved September 1, 2015, from TED talks: http://www.ted.com

Zimbardo, P. (2007). *The lucifer effect: Understanding how good people turn evil.* New York, New York: Random House.

Zukav, G. (1989). *The seat of the soul.* New York, NY: Simon & Schuster.